Seek the Silences
with Thomas Merton

Seek the Silences
with Thomas Merton

Reflections on Identity, Community and Transformative Action

Charles R. Ringma

Published in Great Britain in 2003
Society for Promoting Christian Knowledge
Holy Trinity Church
Marylebone Road
London NW1 4DU

British Library Cataloguing-in-Publication Data

A catalogue record for this book is available from
the British Library

ISBN 0-281-05604-8

1 3 5 7 9 10 8 6 4 2

Typeset by FiSH Books, London WC1
Printed in Great Britain by Bookmarque Ltd,
Croydon, Surrey

For
Athena and Marina

Contents

Preface

The major part of this book was written during my years in the Philippines lecturing at Asian Theological Seminary – a graduate institution serving the whole of South-East Asia – and being a part of Servants to Asia's Urban Poor – a mission committed to incarnational and holistic ministry to Asia's poor living in the slums of major urban centres. Although, from the very beginning, the book had a wider and also a Western audience in view.

The task of forming and empowering urban practitioners who were committed to evangelism and the work of justice, church planting and community development, was the constant challenge. But connected to all of that was the pressing question of sustainability. And that was linked to the much deeper issue that has to do with the motivational centre out of which we all live, work and serve.

These matters bring together the interrelated themes of this book – who I am before God, who I join with in community, and the way in which I engage the world in loving service and prophetic challenge. Or to put that differently, it brings together the themes of being and doing, and those of spirituality and service.

While these matters could be treated in a systematic way, I have chosen a different format, that of short reflective pieces of writing. There are several reasons for this. The first is that a systematic treatment of these themes would involve writing a major text. Since many Christians who seek to integrate faith and life, spirituality and service and being and doing unfortunately do not take the time to read systematic theology, I hope this format will serve such Christians well. Second, the main thrust of this book is not simply informational but also motivational, not simply theological but also reflective. It is written in the hope that you the reader can connect with these reflective pieces as you seek to live in the embrace of God, in the joy and pain of being part of the Christian community and as you seek to serve in your family, neighbourhood and places of work and in the wider society.

What all of this suggests is that I have in view a much broader range of readers than simply those who are training for the formal ministry in the Church and those who are seeking to bring about change in the places of injustice, poverty and marginalization. For whether we work in these areas, or in the marketplace or in the home, we all wrestle with the themes of being and doing and spirituality and service. We are all called to live our life with and before God and with others. We are all called to be nurtured by God and to serve the neighbour. Who we are, what Christ is calling us to be, how we join with others and how we engage in bringing about change and transformation is the challenge facing all of us.

The fact that we are all called to walk a similar journey is amply exemplified in the life of the conversation partner of this book – Thomas Merton. For while he lived much of his life as a monk 'isolated' from the world, Merton nevertheless engaged the world in significant ways. Moreover, his monastic experience with its rhythm of liturgical prayer, the practice of solitude, the experience of community and the value of daily work is in principle not a highly exclusive form of life. What the monk does in a more intentional way, we are all called to be. We too need to live with God, disengage from the daily pressures of life, deepen in a life of prayer and devotion, join more fully in communities of faith and engage the world in such a way that we call it back to the shalom of God's kingdom.

In recognizing the particular circumstances in which I began to write this book and the particular groups of people I was working with, and furthermore acknowledging the particularity of my own journey of faith, community and mission, as well as that of Thomas Merton, I nevertheless believe that here are universal themes. Prayer and service, worship and politics, and contemplation and mission are issues for the Church in Asia, in the West, and in other areas of the globe. I hope you will engage these reflections not as end statements but as conversational pieces. This book is an invitation to reflective dialogue.

Merton is only a conversation partner. I make no attempt to systematically portray his thoughts. These reflections of mine nevertheless resonate with many of Merton's concerns, as I trust they will link with your concerns as well.

It should be noted that this more personal and reflective style of writing was also used by Merton and was perhaps best expressed in his classic *New Seeds of Contemplation*. And so I trust that you will use this book in the quiet place in order to receive grace and encouragement for the journey we must all make and the life of service we must all live.

Throughout these pages you will gain some sense of what has been formative in my own life. Many places, persons and institutions have shaped my inner world and its values and have ordered my life in its social engagement. I am a grateful recipient of much. I am the unworthy child of a gracious God and a less than obedient servant of the Kingdom. So this is at best but a meagre offering. But one that has not been done alone. There are two people to whom I am particularly grateful. Prof. Athena Gorospe gave much valuable feedback and Marina Ringma-McLaren did all of the computer work. To them this book is gratefully dedicated.

Finally, I wish to make a comment about the title of this book. *Seek the Silences* is not a call to a spirituality that draws us to God, but removes us from the pain, needs and challenges of our world. This title does not envision an ascent to God that no longer seeks to wash the feet of the world. Thus this book does not simply have an inward spirituality in view. This is clear from the subtitles with their emphasis not only on being, but also on community and social engagement through transformative action. But the title does highlight that we need to be still before God in order to hear and then do. We need to disengage in order to be empowered. We need to be embraced in order to serve. Or to put all of that differently, mission comes from contemplation.

Charles Ringma
Regent College, Vancouver

Introduction

One of the characteristics of those who think in Western categories is to celebrate the notion of either/or. Influenced by rationalism and driven by the need to make the world manageable and productive, Westerners have been adept at the art of control and categorization.

While these notions and impulses have been important in making our lives and our societies more efficient, this has come at a painful price. Efficiency and productivity lead to specialization and ironically specialization leads to fragmentation. That we live fragmented lives in dysfunctional neighbourhoods is everywhere writ large in our urbanscape. Even our carefully structured social institutions, including the political, educational and medical, are groaning under the strain of economic rationalism and a general cynicism.

There has always been something generally wrong with our world. Sociologically it has always been a divided world between the powerful and those who are powerless. Theologically we understand this as the result of the fall. Human rebellion against God has led to inner fragmentation, social disharmony and the abuse of the created order.

But there is also something particularly wrong with our world and specifically with the First World. This world, which was once formed by a theological vision, is now shaped by an individualistic humanism and materialism. Having thrown off the 'chains' of Christendom, the contemporary world is now struggling in finding its way in the morass of relativism. And now that the 'certainties' of science are found to be equally wanting and problematical, we find ourselves halting at the edges of cynicism and paralysis.

The Christian communities of faith, by and large, have not been able to resist the powerful cultural forces of our time.

Fragmentation, institutional ineptness and uncertainty are common features. Not only do the churches find themselves more and more at the periphery of society, but many Christians are ecclesiastical orphans in the churches they still inhabit. As consumers of religious services they have little stake in and commitment to the religious institutions of which they are a part.

The way forward for the Church, weakened as it is and existing in a difficult environment, is less than clear. The way back to a 'golden age' is not possible. Not only has such an age never existed, but a return to the Christendom model is no longer an option. Moreover, this model must not be repeated in the future. In a world where the Church has too much power and where Church and society reinforce each other, the Church becomes a far cry from a servant, witness and sacrament of the reign of God.

Nor can the Church simply turn inward. While the temptation to isolation and self-protection becomes particularly acute in times of difficulty, it remains true that the inward looking Church becomes a dying Church. The Church was never meant to live for itself. Moreover, it was never called to be self-protective. Nor can it live being afraid of the world. Instead, the community of faith is ever called to live as agents of transformation in our world.

It is also not possible for the Church to live simply for the future. It cannot be marking time waiting for God's eschatological future. It cannot wait for new heavens and a new earth while neglecting its calling to be light, salt and leaven in our world.

Instead, the Church needs to embrace its present vulnerabilities and difficulties. It needs to see itself as the 'little flock' or the 'people in the diaspora', or 'pilgrims on the journey'. The Church needs to accept its present refugee status and marginalization. In this difficult terrain, it may enter the experience of the 'desert' and accept its corporate 'dark night' of the soul.

None of this is to suggest that the Church must see itself as abandoned by God. God is faithful in his covenant love for his people and in his equally great love for the whole world. But the God of the Bible has never been the God who baptizes particular historical conditions or particular institutional realities of the Church. Moreover, God purges his people and teaches them to trust him in the desert.

It is within this broad framework of thought that *Seek the Silences with Thomas Merton* has been written. Even though it was partly written in Asia, it in many ways has the Church in the first world in view. At its heart, this series of reflections calls us to a more vulnerable spirituality. It invites us to cry out to God, rather than to articulate the certainties of faith. It calls us first of all to contemplation before calling us to action. And more centrally, it calls us to a discerning faith that names the idols of our world and resists their power.

It will become evident that this book calls us into the slow march of God. We cannot readily fix our churches or transform our world. In the midst of faithful service, we are invited to wait for God. In our busy lives, we are called to solitude. In the fracturing praxis of independent individualism, we are called to Christian community. In our fearful presence in the world, we are called to bold and holistic service.

The themes of this book are self-evident. We note the importance of the individual, but reject individualism. We do not understand the person in holy isolation, but as a person in relationship first with the Creator and Redeemer and then with each other in friendship and community. Furthermore, we wish to emphasize that while friendship and community are to be valued in and of themselves, they cannot be self-seeking and inward-oriented. The blessings of community are gifts to be shared with the world.

Seek the Silences embodies the invitation to hearing before doing, silence before speaking, aloneness before community, crying before prophesying. On its pages is no grand plan for Christian reconstruction. But here are familiar themes of the fragility of faith and the certainty of God's grace, the vulnerability of our spirituality and the power of God's Spirit, the weakness of our communities of faith and the faithfulness of God's covenant love.

In these pages, you will find not so much the certainties of faith, but the celebration of the mystery of the God who is with us in the midst of our journey of faith in a world that has relegated God to the realm of the superstitious. So, rather than bold pronouncements, here are the cries and whispers of faith made in the presence of the God of surprises.

Introducing Thomas Merton

An introduction is a most curious activity. One introduces a particular person to another by making some salient comments about the one being introduced. This is meant to help the person to whom the introduction is made to situate the one being introduced and to know something helpful or relevant about the person.

The one doing the introduction acts as a sort of go-between for the introducee as well as the person to whom the introduction is made. In a complex hermeneutic, the introducee then makes certain comments, provides a certain amount of information, even gives certain metaphorical signals that say something that is useful.

That this shorthand activity is riddled with difficulties is rather obvious. The introducer may not represent the introducee very well. The one to whom the person is being introduced may not find the introduction helpful, either because he or she knows nothing about the person and so what is said is not all that helpful, or because he or she may know the introducee much better than the introducer.

Recognizing these difficulties in day-to-day face-to-face relationships is one thing. But these difficulties become compounded in introducing a prolific writer to unknown readers.

Nevertheless, there are some things I should say about Thomas Merton. But let me first make some qualifications. The brief chronology on Merton at the back of this book can be consulted for some basic information about his life and writings. In the secondary bibliography there are a number of biographies that one may wish to read. But most importantly, Merton best introduces himself. There are his autobiographical books such as *The Seven Storey Mountain* and *The Sign of Jonas* among others, as well as the publication of his journals and diaries and his extensive correspondence (see the brief chronology on Merton where these volumes are listed).

Through these intensely personal writings, but also through his poetry and other books, Merton wants us to know him in his struggles and issues of faith as well as his ideas, concerns and vision for living the Christian life in solitude, community and service to the world.

There are many different windows through which one may view Merton. One is through the window of religious conversion. How did this secular and urbane young man with his literary interests become enamoured with the Roman Catholic faith to the point that this faith began to define his entire life direction? And more specifically, how did he become interested in becoming a Roman Catholic monk.

Another window is the psychological interest. Given Thomas Merton's childhood experiences of loss of first his mother and then his father, given much geographical rootlessness in his younger years, and given some of the folly of his youth, can this help us to understand his dramatic choices, his writing interests and the role he sought to play both in the Trappist monastery and in the wider issues of his time?

A further interest, basically sociological in nature, is to understand Merton in the larger social and cultural currents of his time. To what extent was he a product of the events of the postwar period through to the turbulent 1960s in the USA. And to what extent did this help to shape his interests and concerns as a religious contemplative, who, unlike many of his fellow monks, had access to the significant literature of his time?

And then of course there are the more fragmenting interests where one divides Merton into various functions. Thus we can look at Merton the writer, or, more specifically, the poet. Or we may look at Merton the contemplative. Or the social activist. Or the person involved in inter-religious dialogue.

It should be fairly obvious, however, that one should attempt to understand a person as holistically as possible. All these windows contribute to an attempt to understand and to appreciate. But to focus on an aspect of a person's activity may not get us very far in our appreciation of that person.

My own reading of Merton suggests some of the following perspectives. Merton was both an intellectually capable and a fundamentally creative person. The former observation is evident from the breadth and depth of his theological, spiritual and social concerns. While he was not a systematic theologian, his writings on spirituality and his skills in inter-religious dialogical reflection are significant. His creativity is evident in his writing style, poetry and use of the paintbrush and camera. For his creative writing style, see particularly his *Raids on the Unspeakable*.

Furthermore, Merton was a deeply contemplative person. This is evident not only from his participation in a Trappist monastery and later in his life in a hermitage in the Abbey grounds, but in the fundamental orientation of his being. Merton did not only participate in the contemplative practices of his religious community, but sought to deepen these practices in his own lifestyle and experience. His extensive writings on contemplation, of which *Contemplative Prayer* is one of his finer works, came not only out of his communal experience, but out of rereading the tradition of spirituality. Moreover, Merton sought to live in openness and attentiveness to God, his own inner needs and strivings, his community, the world of nature which he loved so deeply, and the issues of his time.

There is nothing of a settled nature about Merton. He is both experimental and reformist. The former is evident in the development of his writing style and his writing interests which ranged from monasticism, spirituality, fiction and poetry to social critique and inter-religious dialogue. It is further evidenced in his openness to people of other traditions and perspectives, He is not only interested in a Karl Barth and a Gandhi, but also in a James Joyce and an Albert Camus. He explores Eastern Orthodoxy as well as Zen Buddhism. The latter, the reformist, is evident in Merton's concern to deepen his own monastic tradition, to see the Roman Catholic Church become more open to the currents and issues of the contemporary world, and to see Christians resist the injustices of their world. As such, we may say that Merton was a prophetic voice in his time.

What is striking about Merton is his deep aloneness. This despite his life in monastic community and his wide circle of friends. Merton's extant letters alone run into five volumes. This aloneness made him long for and eventually succeed in gaining permission to live in a hermitage within the Abbey grounds. My understanding of this dimension of Merton's life is that this was the source that nurtured his relationship with God, opened him to the visits of his friends and provided the fuel out of which he wrote. The extensive pouring out of words in books, poems, reflections and letters came from this lonely place.

It is clear that Merton never saw himself as a centrally located person. He had no desire to become the Abbot of his community. Instead, he saw himself as a person on the margins. The outsider on the inside. This lonely place is not the place of proud distanciation or sullen self-pity. Instead, it is the place of critical reflection and engagement. On the margins of society and even within his own community, particularly because of his stance on certain socio-political issues, Merton was able to engage the issues within monastic communities and the wider society with creative and prophetic insight. This made him the traveller on a frequently lonely road.

My engagement with Merton in this book, while in the light of the above, is specifically from the perspective that Merton did not simply make his monastic journey for the benefit of monasticism. He had a much wider audience in view. While he particularizes monastic spirituality, prayer, solitude and community, he constantly adds that these dimensions are in some way relevant for all Christians.

While we are not all called to become monks, we are all called to Christian vocation and to the art of relinquishment and the pain of asceticism. While we are not all called to liturgical prayer, we are all called to the intimacy of prayer. While we are not all called to a monastic community, we are all called to friendship, Christian community and human solidarity. While we are not all called to become poets, we are called to use our creativity for the purposes of the kingdom of God and for the well-being of human community.

Merton offers us, in his extensive writings and through his journals, a window into a particular way of being a Christian and living the Christian life. This distinctiveness acts as a mirror for us. In the face of the other we may see things about ourselves to which we otherwise might be blind. It is out of this perspective that I have written *Seek the Silences with Thomas Merton*.

And this has been done for very good reasons. Just as Merton engaged Buddhism to reflect more deeply on his monastic tradition, so I have engaged Merton to reflect more deeply on Protestant and more specifically on evangelical spirituality and praxis.

My reading of Merton convinces me that Thomas remained firmly embedded within the Roman Catholic faith in spite of his inter-religious interests. I have no intent to repeat or justify every aspect of that faith tradition. But I am interested in exploring the way in which Merton challenges me to live my faith more prayerfully and authentically.

And this brings me to the heart of this series of reflections. Merton is no plaster saint. His falling in love with a nurse, which caused him temporarily to question his vocation, illustrates his humanity and vulnerability. He tells us of the stirrings of the Spirit and the struggles of faith. His quest for union with God and his sinfulness. His longing for ultimacy and his engagement of the critical issues of his time.

Merton invites us to embrace an incarnational spirituality. A faith that loves God and cares for the neighbour. A prayer life that longs for eschatological intimacy, but embraces a political awareness and social engagement.

While Merton may not hold a whole lot of specific answers for us, the broad brush strokes of his life and ministry remind us of some of the contours of Christian spirituality: the Christian life is God's miraculous work in us; it is sustained by the love of God, the work of the Spirit and a eucharistic fellowship; the Trinitarian God invites us into community with himself, with each other and with the wider society; God invites us to asceticism and relinquishment and to the practice of prayer and solitude, for in the empty place we receive God's bounties; and finally, the God who invites us to intimacy and contemplation is the God who calls us to the world and to heal its pain and to resist and challenge its idolatries.

At heart, Merton does not call us to the spirituality of the oasis, but to an exodus spirituality which in faith walks the lonely road that knows the shame and pain of Golgotha as well as the miracle of Pentecost.

BEING
The Search for Self-Identity

Who we are as humans is not unproblematical. In many ways we are a mystery to ourselves, and our ability to understand others is not without its difficulties. This is not only true of people from other cultures, but may also be true of people as close to home as our parents, spouse or children.

The fact that we are different from others plays an important part. Gender, personality, cultural, linguistic and occupational differences are all significant factors. But the fact that I continue to be a mystery to myself should signal that I should not be surprised by the mystery that I find in others.

While it is true that the various sciences, including the biological, psychological and sociological, have helped in our self-understanding, most of us continue to struggle with ourselves. Our sense of identity, rather than being secure, deep and strong, is often fragile and vulnerable.

In many ways, our contemporary culture has not helped us. It has tended to magnify the autonomous self and the productive self. The former fragments the fundamental need for relationality. The latter dynamites our spirituality and the need for renewal and empowerment.

Moreover, the complexity of our urbanscape has filtered into our soulscape. Belonging to many primary, secondary and tertiary communities we are ever pulled in various directions. Family, the workplace, the neighbourhood, recreational activities, church involvement and wider commitments to society all vie for time and attention. Little wonder that we experience ourselves as the fragmented self.

The biblical story invites us to see the human person within a framework very different from the values of contemporary culture. It begins by accenting that we are not the accidents of history, but are the result of God's creative activity making us women and men in God's likeness and image. Moreover, in spite of our folly and sin that rent apart the fabric of God's good design, God continues to care for and renew his creation. This brings us into the realm of God's grace where we are loved for who we are in the love of God.

In Scripture, our identity is not simply the sum total of our biological inheritance, our family history and our own strivings and achievements. It is more fundamentally formed in relation to the great Lover who both affirms and renews us.

Thomas Merton throughout his writings wrestles with the question of our identity. He is particularly concerned about the way in which our contemporary culture shapes us in terms of independence, success, productivity and power and control. He believes that these values shape a false self. The truer self knows and embraces difficulty and disappointment and not only success. It knows the blessing of contemplation and not simply the skill of productivity. It celebrates relationship with God and others and not only the gift of individuation. Moreover, it knows the journey of vulnerability and not only the deadly and frequently empty road of power.

While the search for self-identity has its scripted elements in that we need to accept and embrace what we have been given from our family of origin, it also has its open dimensions. We are persons in the process of becoming. We make choices regarding love, career and life direction which contour the texture of our lives. We grow through our responses to difficulty, pain and disappointment. And we experience the disjunctures and surprises in our lives which give us unsought qualities.

None of this in any way suggests that who we are becomes nicely clear. While we may be thankful for what is secure, doubts, insecurities and vulnerability will continue to plague us. And the mystery of life and personhood will continue to frame much of our existence.

Who we are is finally a matter not of a science that quantifies us, but of a love that qualifies us. It is not a matter of certainty, but a journey of faith. It has little to do with self-preoccupation, but everything to do with self-giving. It is more a matter of being given and receiving than it is a matter of self-doing. As such, it is a journey frought with pitfalls and possibilities.

Becoming

The painful journey of growth

While the time of childhood is usually one of acceptance, particularly when one lives in secure relationships, that all changes in adolescence. This is the time of self-discovery and struggle with who we are and what life is all about. While some of this struggle may come to rest as we make helpful transitions into meaningful relationships and work, we continue to wrestle with the way we are and the way we are becoming.

These questions are usually not to the fore when things are going well and we appear to make a success of things. They tend to emerge in the difficult and in the transitional phases of our lives. They barge into our consciousness particularly when we thought we were doing well but had to face unexpected criticism, disregard or even rejection. At such times, we discover how fragile the self really is and how much it depends on external affirmation and approval.

Yet, sooner or later, we do need to come to terms with our more naked self. This is not to suggest that we ever see the self fully naked. Such ultimate and blinding insight is usually denied us, and just as well, for that may be all too much for us. But the self stripped of some of its defences and illusions can swim into view in times of crisis, the place of contemplation and revelation, times of dislocation and settings where we are confronted with something or someone other than the familiar.

Merton in many of his writings speaks of the need to move beyond the social self to the authentic self. Later, he came to the realization that 'there is after all no hidden mysterious "real self"'.[1] In other words, while a self shaped only by the dominant values of our culture, and functioning only for society's affirmation, is an inadequate way of being, this does not suggest that the authentic self can be found by some stripping-away process. The metaphor cannot be one of corn and husk.

There is no intact real self that awaits self-discovery. There is only the self and its painful transformations. In the ebb and flow of life, in moments of ecstasy and despair, in times of acceptance and rejection and in the movements of grace and emptiness, we may experience a growing awareness of who we are. What our strengths and weaknesses are, what our more important values are and what vocational choices we wish to explore, all join into the mix of our development.

In this complex process, there are likely to be life-giving moments, insights and decisions, as well as death-dealing detours which will call us to further renewal and transformation. Here there are no road maps. And no-one can make this journey for us. This is the trek of life we all must make, and final success will be denied us.

All of this is not to suggest that we make this journey alone. Loved ones and companions on the journey, while they can only be our tentative guides, can make the journey easier. We need bread and water in the desert. And in the deserts of our deepest self-questioning and uncertainty we need others to be there for us, not in their strength but in their vulnerable availability.

In the midst of life
The gentle journey of discovery

I have met people in the secular world and in Christian ministry who gallantly rode the fiery stallion of control. They not only sought to control their own lives and destiny, but also pulled others into the vortex of their own visions and paranoia and inflexibility. These fevered dreamings of the authoritarian personality did not make the world more manageable. Instead, it ultimately brought havoc and chaos.

Since life is bigger than all of us, we have to learn its gentle lessons and fit in to its persistent rhythms. We don't stand outside of life so that we can control it. We are embedded in it. We are thrown into the world. We can foolishly try to carry life or wisely allow it to sustain us and carry us along.

None of this means that we should be passive or fatalistic. Nor should we renege on our God-given task to rule, shape and care for our world. It certainly does not mean that we allow others to make important life choices for us without our active participation and involvement. Nor does it mean that we live haphazardly, going along with whatever comes our way or takes our fancy. Learning to live life's lessons has nothing to do with being irresponsible.

Merton reminds us that 'the mystery of life can only be known by being lived'.[2] Put differently, many paths are made by walking. Or differently again, in the reality of being loved and being loving, we begin to understand the nature of love.

The gentle meanings of life are not found through critical distance, but through immersion. And since life cannot be lived against itself, we have to live within the realities of our own giftedness, the blessing of family, the reality of community and the givenness of our world. We should neither subvert our biological clock nor frustrate our personality. We need to accept the burdens and the challenges of increasing responsibility and be gentle with ourselves in the ageing process and the dimunition of our powers.

If we live and reflect, act and pray, create and celebrate, then life itself will be meaningful even in the midst of pain and struggle.

Taking oneself lightly
Learning to depend on God's care and sustenance

I am sure you have met them. The happily fat, rollicking, easy-going and joyful people of this world. They don't take things too seriously and generally manage to have a good time.

I am not one of them. I belong to the other end of the spectrum: much too serious, focused and compulsive. I work on three major projects at the same time, read ten books at once and complain that I am too busy. Those who are close to me no longer listen to my complaints because they know I have only myself to blame.

All my life I have struggled to find ways to be more gentle with myself. I would be lying if I claimed that I had found solutions.

It seems that I am not alone in this struggle. Merton writes, 'we cripple our own spirit by taking ourselves too seriously. We expect too much from ourselves when we ought to expect everything from God on whom we utterly depend.'[3]

I am sure that the reasons for such drivenness lie deeply embedded in one's psyche and that one's early family development had something to do with all of this. But I am not planning a personal archaeological expedition. Rather, let me tell you something of my faltering journey to take life and myself a little more easily.

The first thing I have learned to do is to slot into my busy life those things that I love doing. For me, these are learning and writing, particularly poetry. Doing both energizes me. I am sure you have your own ways of being energized.

Second, I love being with people I am close to. A number of intimate friendships are very important to me. And nothing takes priority over time together.

Third, life's reality cruelly teaches us that one cannot do everything and that we need to do what we do best, playing our strengths and using our gifts. This helps us to focus and to say 'no' to things that are outside of our ability or expertise.

And finally and most importantly, there is the ongoing challenge to imbibe God's gentle care for us. The God who calls us to creative and responsible activity is also the God who calls us to sabbath celebration, to cease from our labours, to rejoice in God's goodness and to enjoy the fruit of our hands.

Even the walk of costly discipleship is not without the blessing of God's care, the gift of Christian community and the solidarity of brothers and sisters in Christ, the celebration of bread and wine and the unexpected blessings of the God of surprises.

The mystery of growth
Making progress when you least expect it

I know of people who have been ever so faithful in the practice of their faith; in church attendance; participating in the sacraments; and in service. But they are so dull, rigid and often so immature.

Others I know are almost the opposite. They are erratic in their faithfulness; have wandered down far too many side alleys; have frequently repented and yet are full of the milk of human kindness.

It just doesn't make sense! In fact, so much of life and even our experience of faith does not make sense.

Merton echoes something of this mystery. He writes, 'I know too that somehow my interior life is deeper and that I have more peace and that I am closer to God and more under his control. But do not ask me how I got there because I do not know.'[4]

I can re-echo this mystery.

There were times when things were going so well, both in ministry and in building community. And before we knew what was happening, zeal and fruitfulness were diminishing and the glue of community had come unstuck. Everything looked so good and appeared to be so strong, but somehow the rot had set in.

Conversely, when we were naive and spontaneous, struggling, experimental and often not very clear about what we were doing, the magic of the Spirit and God's undeserved blessings were with us.

These kinds of incidents can be multiplied.

On reflection, God has a strange way of working which most often cuts across the way we think things should work. And this strange way has everything to do with the mystery of grace.

God has glee in turning things around. God loves to catch us by surprise. God enjoys giving undeserved blessings.

God does not seem to be all that impressed with our great efforts, our much doing and our neatly thought-out and executed projects. This does not mean that God blesses lethargy and rejoices over our lack of forethought and planning.

But God appears to be with us much more when we are vulnerable than when we are strong, and when we are prayerful than when we think we are doing so well.

This is also true of our own spiritual growth. We grow strong not so much through self-effort, but through the unexpected blessings that come our way.

Acceptance
Celebrating the way God has made us

I think we live life locked on the horns of a dilemma. There are
things we must accept. There are other things we must resist and
transcend. And we need so much wisdom to know which is which.

Merton tells us that 'it is humility to accept our humanity, pride
to reject it'.[5] Clearly he is emphasizing that each of us must come to
terms with both the possibilities and limitations of our
creatureliness. And that we need to rejoice in the talents, gifts and
abilities that God has given us. To reject our humanity is ultimately
to reject God's good gifts.

But there is more to the story.

There are also things about ourselves that we may not accept.
While we accept God's handiwork in our lives, we reject all that
which has marred and twisted us and has made us less than what
God desires us to be.

Sadly, at best, we are flawed. This is not God's doing. It is often
through our wilfulness and stubbornness, and ultimately our
disobedience to the will of God that things get messed up. But the
faultlines in our lives are not only our own doing. We come from
less than ideal families and are socialized into cultural and societal
values which are far from constructive.

Surprisingly, we don't start by rejecting the hurting parts of
ourselves and denying the faultlines, let alone by rationalizing our
disobedience. We start by accepting both the good and the bad in
our lives. The good we celebrate, protect and enhance. For the good
we are truly thankful. The not-so-good we face with sadness and
humility, looking to God to help us in the journey of transformation.

To look to God for help does not mean that we do nothing
ourselves. While God desires the best for us, we cannot cling to what
should be changed. Therefore we need to let go. We need to mourn
our failures and turn away from the things that are less than good.
In repentance we look to God to empower us to live and respond in
more constructive ways.

In so doing, we embrace the grace of God and the mysterious
work of his Spirit. We accept that our hope lies with the Lord our

God. And that God will join us in the fray as we seek to become more fully human by being more attuned to his will.

A *winsome humility*

Gaining a truer perspective of ourselves

I have met both kinds of people. I am sure you have as well – those who are so full of themselves and their own abilities and achievements that the sin of pride triumphs in their presence, and those who are so humble that they have become innocuous non-persons. I am not sure which is the greater tragedy, but clearly the former will make a more powerful impact on our world, although not necessarily for the better.

Between these two extremes lies a very different kind of person. One that I am striving to be and one that you may also find attractive and challenging. I am talking about a person who is secure and strong and proactive, who dares to take life in full stride, but who at the same time acknowledges a deep dependence on God's grace and enablement.

Merton makes the comment that 'the only way to possess... [God's] greatness is to pass through the needle's eye of your own absolute insufficiency'.[6] This does not mean that for God to be great we are to be nothing. Nor does it mean that we should celebrate our insufficiencies and inabilities. Since a grovelling self-negation can hardly bring glory to God, something quite different is spoken of here.

I believe that we are face to face with the challenge that if we want to do God's good in our families, neighbourhoods, churches and world, then we need to possess the grace and love of God in our own lives. Since being and doing are related, we can only live to God's glory when we are possessed by God.

To live before God in openness and humility means that our own prowess and self-sufficiency have to be radically curtailed and transformed. There are no easy formulas for this kind of inner surgery. But somehow we need to learn the lesson that our best, let alone our worst, does not achieve God's good in our world.

To be dependent on God does not mean that we become inactive and passive. It actually means the opposite. We still exert ourselves. We still strive and work hard. But we embed our activities in prayer and our zeal and strength we draw from God.

To live in this way is never easy. We easily become self-reliant, and even our humility can become pride. But when we cry to the Lord as those needing help, God will surely rush to our aid.

Seeking the silences
Nature's gift of renewal

I have lived in cities all my life. The largest and most crowded was Metro Manila. Cities are the centres of power, business, culture and education. My reason for being there had nothing to do with these things. For me, the city was the place for ministry and service.

But my commitment to incarnational ministry in the city did not mean that I could wholeheartedly embrace everything in the city and its way of life. I also needed to escape from time to time.

Thomas Merton writes, 'my heart was filled with a kind of longing to breathe the air of that lonely valley and to listen to its silence'.[7] My experience was similar. A day in the mountains with its tropical rainforests, its clean air and its awesome vistas was like crystal clear water to a parched tongue.

But what was most refreshing was the silence of the brooding craggy mountain tops wrapped in vapour shroud and the womb valleys like a haunted abyss infinitely out of reach and yet insistently inviting.

While refreshment comes most simply in the blessing of sleep at day's end and more specifically in the place of prayer and solitude, nature is also God's special gift of renewal. And it is there, waiting. It asks no special rituals and incantations. It simply beckons us to enter.

Nature, especially when untouched by human hand, has a way of overwhelming us by its sheer beauty, diversity and primitiveness. Everywhere it witnesses to the awesome power of God.

While there are those who are renewed by people contact, introverts who gain their energy from within themselves are especially blessed by silence. Although nature invites the outward gaze, its silence also encourages an inward reflection.

In the grandeur of nature we re-experience our own smallness. In the beauty of nature we come to acknowledge the limitations and imperfections of the urban habitat that we have made. And in the silence of nature we worship the God who has made all things well and who invites us to enjoy the beauty of his handiwork.

While there are the mountains of terror which disgorge their innermost being, there are also the mountains of steady stability which remind us of the steadfastness of the Lord, our God.

Attachment and detachment
The art of gaining ground through a little dying

Most of us are familiar with the imagery of the clenched fist and the open hand. The one suggests a defiant holding on, while the other symbolizes the gentle art of relinquishment.

It is one thing to be enamoured with the verbal imagery. It is quite another to live the metaphor.

Both attachment and detachment bring their respective blessings, challenges and difficulties. Attachment has to do with entry and joining. Here connectedness flows over into commitment. Here we find the reality of community and solidarity.

Detachment, on the other hand, has to do with letting go, leaving and relinquishment. Although a certain amount of detachment is necessary even within the midst of community lest we lose our identity in the group, detachment is the freeing but difficult process of letting go in order to be available for new opportunities.

Neither is necessarily easy. To come and to go may be equally difficult. Both also have their particular blessings.

Merton in speaking of contemplation identifies these two movements. He writes, 'there are always two aspects: the positive one, by which we are united to God in love, and the negative one, by which we are detached and separated from everything that is not God'.[8]

The need to hold on or to let go is sometimes very straightforward. To cleave to the good and to reject evil sounds simple enough, except that sometimes to know which is which is not that self-evident.

What is not so simple is the art of holding on and letting go at the same time. I may need to work on maintaining a particular relationship, but need to let go of certain expectations and demands so that the friendship can achieve a new level of depth and purpose.

Sadly, we so often hold but crush, or relinquish but abandon. To hold what is good and to let go what is unhelpful or undesirable requires more than mere discernment. It requires an abandonment to the God who both holds us fast and shelters and nurtures us and who empowers and releases us.

Falling into conversation
The rivulets of enlightenment

I am quite sure you have had similar experiences, when a particular conversation somehow magically moves into a whole new dimension.

It matters not that the conversation is with a long-term friend or a recent acquaintance. Nor is the topic under discussion particularly important. It doesn't need to be a deep philosophical discussion for the magic to begin.

A good conversation, where neither party is seeking to control the agenda, has a to-and-fro movement. The one thing can lead to another and one will probably end up talking about something quite different from where the conversation began. And things may be discussed which have a revelatory quality.

I am, of course, not talking about the conversation of business or planning meetings. They are driven by different concerns. To deal with the agenda. To get the job done. I wonder whether more would get done if the above dimension could be allowed for! But sadly, when the priests of industry are concocting the economic grail, the voice of the prophet is seldom heard, even though it is necessary.

So I am talking about conversations between friends, lovers and even strangers. Conversations that occur informally and spontaneously and move beyond social niceties to the opening of heart and mind. These conversations can also occur between a teacher and a student, a mentor and mentee, between peers, and in a small group involved in a brainstorming session.

The magic can also occur in a Bible discussion group where insights are shared that open up whole new ways of understanding the mystery of faith and our walk with God and our neighbours.

Merton makes the comment, one can say 'more than he knows and more than he means'.[9]

While new insights can come in many ways – through careful research, hard thinking, gentle reflection, intuitive perception and dreams – they also occur in the art of conversation.

Not only can we hear new things from others, but also from ourselves. It is usually the latter that is the biggest surprise.

In conversations we fall into language. But not into a monologue. True conversation is dialogical. It is the magic of partnership and participation. And, therefore, conversation has the possibility of pulling us beyond ourselves. Away from the familiar into the unknown. Away from the prosaic into the mysterious. We move from the known into the revelatory.

In conversations of this kind we may re-tap ancient veins, suspended thoughts and unresolved issues. The unprocessed galvanizes into clear concepts. The subterranean becomes luminous.

I believe the Spirit of God has much to do with this undeserved magic.

The travellers on the Emmaus road fell into conversation with the risen Christ, and very ordinary talk became revelatory and transformative.

In a world not only of secular chatter, but of so much religious rhetoric as well, may we know the art of conversation that brings new inspiration to our dull lives!

At-homeness

The gift of inner peace

Maybe my upbringing, or possibly the fact that I am an introvert, has something to do with the reality that I enjoy being by myself. This was already so from a very early age. I begged my parents to allow me to sleep in the attic. I spent most afternoons after school wandering in the nearby fields. And the punishment of being consigned to the dark cellar was more a gift of solitude.

My coming to faith in Christ and the subsequent spiritual journey did not change the major contours of my existence. I was happy to be part of the Church and even lived in intentional Christian community, but I was most happy to be by myself.

This orientation had nothing to do with a sense of arrogance nor with a sense of inadequacy. I did not see myself above others, nor did I have problems relating to others. Hence my happiness with aloneness did not spring from difficulties, but from the very core of who I am as a person.

All the calls from the pulpit about the importance of quiet time sounded rather strange to me. Why was there so much emphasis on this as if it was something that people were not doing? And who would not want to spend time by themselves in reflection and prayer?

It seems to me that to be 'at home' with oneself is a great gift. This is not something we can manufacture, but can only receive. But it seems to be a rare gift. Many people seem to be inwardly disconnected, or even more strongly put, inwardly discontented. To this Merton alludes when he notes, 'if we have no hope of being at peace with ourselves in our personal loneliness and silence...we will keep running and never stop'.[10]

Now that I am much older, the desire for aloneness has increased. This is understandable. The ageing process makes us more reflective.

And contemplation rather than action becomes for many the more dominant focus. Sadly, for many this is a late discovery rather than the normal pattern of their lives.

So what does the blessing of faith have to do with these matters? For me, faith did not turn me to the practice of solitude. That was naturally a part of my life. But faith did change the purpose of my solitude. It was now a matter no longer of simply being by myself, but of being alone in the presence of God.

This deepened my sense of 'at-homeness'. To be 'at home' with oneself, one's setting and environment and also to be with God makes for a richly textured solitude that does not drive us to a despairing loneliness, but to wonderful intimacy and sense of wonder and peace.

What this highlights is that so much is already given to us in the gift of our humanity and in the shaping of our personal biography. Common grace brings us the blessings of being made in God's image and the gift of life. God's redemptive and transforming grace takes nature's gifts and deepens and reorients them. The gifts of our humanity become the signs of God's beneficence. Thus rather than being on the run, we stand still long enough to be loved by the relentless Lover who seeks to make us more fully human.

Facing failure
Learning from our difficulties

I wish that I could say that all my failures have had a redemptive quality. But that is simply not true. From some failures I learned absolutely nothing. Some were quite detrimental. They undermined my self-confidence and sense of well-being.

What is worse, some failures not only had a negative impact on me, but badly affected others. Many incidents readily spring to mind. A repetitive theme was the failure to intervene early enough in problematic situations. But, of course, I have much more glaring failures to my debit column.

It is tantalizingly true, however, that all this can and should be very different. I can learn from my mistakes and I slowly and laboriously have.

Merton makes the observation, 'my infidelity to Christ, instead of making me sick with despair, drives me to throw myself all the more blindly into the arms of his mercy'.[11] What this means is that failure can be positively turned around.

In learning from my mistakes the first lesson simply may be that I need to be far more realistic about what I can and should do. Sometimes, failure is the direct by-product of being over-committed and trying to do too much.

Failure, and particularly repeated failure, may help me to refocus my occupational focus and my general life direction. I may be simply a square peg in a round hole. I may be trying to do things for which I am neither suited nor gifted. If this is the case, failure needs to move me to embrace the courage to try something different.

My failure with myself or others is one thing, but what about my failure with God? Thankfully, this carries the best news of all. For while our failure in relation to others may well lead to relationship breakdown, failure before God can always result in forgiveness, restoration and renewal. In my moment of weakness I can experience God's embrace, the kiss of peace, the healing touch and the empowerment to move forward in order to live again, risk again, love again, try again.

Making mistakes
The call to ongoing conversion

For some people, making mistakes is an unmitigated disaster. It's an affront to their identity and their abilities.

But since we all, sooner or later, make mistakes, people like those above are forever scrambling to find excuses or rationalizations. The problems always lie somewhere else. And since their egos are too immature and fragile to acknowledge personal shortcomings, nothing is ever gained and progress is never made. No bursts of self-insight ever occur out of the ashes of failure and difficulty.

Merton believes that failure can and should be productive. He writes, 'it is by making mistakes that we gain experience, not only for ourselves but for others'.[12]

I believe that many more specific blessings lie embedded in the seeming chaos of our mistakes. This, of course, is not to suggest that mistakes are inherently good. Mistakes are usually bad and many mistakes have produced disastrous consequences for ourselves and often more so for others. But there are redemptive possibilities for mistakes. And learning to make mileage out of our mistakes is a singularly maturing process.

Making mistakes is a reoccurring signal of our humanity. While we are all creatures of great significance and worth, and even though some have great ability and expertise, we are all less than perfect. This gives us our proper definition. God alone is perfect and we are considerably less so. And this less so reality sooner or later expresses itself in everything that we say, do, shape and make. Our humanity, therefore, while wonderfully shaped, is deeply flawed. To believe this is not necessarily to plug into some mediaeval and morbid understanding of sin, it is a simple acknowledgement writ large on everything that we do.

Mistakes can, however, move us. Not to the escapist strategies of rationalization, but to the banquet table of God's grace. Mistakes are the invitation to a humility that acknowledges failure and seeks forgiveness and renewal. Mistakes, therefore, invite us to live in the wide terrain of God's grace rather than in the narrow clefts of our immature egos which always need to be right and therefore always excuse our behaviours.

Now I am not suggesting that mistakes only need grace devoid of responsibility. To make things right, to compensate and make restitution wherever possible are the fruits of grace. These things should be done, but should flow from grace and not from our own attempts to make everything right, because that is often impossible.

But there is so much more embedded in the fabric of our mistakes.

Mistakes are the clarion call to partnership. While failures should draw us to God and to those we have failed, hurt or offended, we should also turn to others for help. Mistakes call for the participation of others. They are the windows of opportunity that take us beyond ourselves into seeking the cooperation of others.

Mistakes and failures therefore need not be the bells that toll the sombre melodies of death. Instead, they can be the wake-up bell inviting us to the personal journey of humility and the corporate journey of partnership.

Receptivity

Learning the more difficult art of receiving

By temperament I am the most independent of all the personality types. My family upbringing undoubtedly had much to do with the way I began to operate in the world.

Coming from a long line of small-town family business people with an underlay and overlay of the Protestant work ethic, the basic motto of life was: Don't look to others, look to yourself; don't depend on others, do it yourself.

In one sense, there is nothing wrong with this approach to life. It encourages self-reliance and entrepreneurship. In another sense, there is everything wrong with this philosophy of life. It can lead to a hardness towards those who are struggling. The attitude towards them is often: You will have to solve your own problems. But this approach to life can also lead to an unwillingness to face our own needs and pain and not to be open to the help and encouragement that others may be able to give us.

Merton puts it this way: 'the things we really need come to us only as gifts, and in order to receive them as gifts we have to be open. In order to be open we have to renounce ourselves, in a sense we have to die to our image of ourselves, our autonomy, our fixation upon our self-willed identity.'[13]

The idea that we can do it by ourselves, and have no need of others, not only is sheer arrogance, but is a falsification of the most basic principle of life – life is a gift. God is the giver of life and most of what we are and have received comes from the graciousness of others whether that be our mother who nurtured us, our father who disciplined us, our teacher who taught us or our friend who encouraged us.

Because we are not complete in ourselves, the gentle genius of life necessitates that others help us where we are needy, and complement us where we are lacking. This most basic reality catapults us towards relationships and community.

The beauty of life lies not in its singularity, but in its complementarity. It is in my willingness to receive and to be enriched by others that I not only will become a better person, but will have more to give to others.

Emptiness

Recognizing a motivational centre-point

For a long time I believed the cliché that ministry comes from overflow, that we give to others out of the fullness that we have received.

While that may be true for some people, I do not believe that it is true of me. I also think that there is a dangerous element in this kind of perspective. It so easily gives the impression that ministry comes out of the strength and the resources that we have. It begs the question whether ministry can also come out of weakness and vulnerability.

Merton is at his paradoxical best when he writes, 'we must live by the strength of an apparent emptiness that is always truly empty and yet never fails to support at every moment'.[14]

I do not want to pontificate on why Merton believes this and lives like this. That it has something to do with his family background, the major contours of his life journey and his faith commitment, is without a doubt. But I do want to acknowledge that this is part of my own experience.

Whenever I spend time with people, counsel someone, preach a sermon, teach a course, complete some project or write a book, I do not feel complete or fulfilled and certainly not self-satisfied. I feel the opposite. I feel empty.

Does that mean that I am unhappy that the project was completed? Certainly not! Does that mean that I am unappreciative of the opportunity to serve in particular ways? Certainly not! But it does mean that I don't feed my ego off the things I have done. They are done with God's help. They are incomplete. They could have been done better. And they are released into God's providential care.

And so I return to my inner world, empty, but full of new possibilities. In the emptiness I find peace and renewal. And the emptiness becomes the fruitful seedbed for new adventures.

A *wholesome* holiness

The gentle art of becoming more fully human

I have had the privilege of meeting many great men and women in business, government and the arts. I have also met many wonderful Christians. Some directly served the Church. Others served God in the marketplace.

But if you were to ask me the question: have I met many holy men or women, I would be baffled indeed. I guess I am not all that sure what such a person would look like, or, more precisely, how such a person would live and act in our world.

I have met Christians who were very pietistic. But they were also very narrow and had embraced a world-denying form of Christianity which failed to enter the pain and injustice of our world. Were they holy?

At the other end of the spectrum, I have also met Christians who have incarnated themselves in the places of degradation in our world, but who know little about prayer and a life of intimacy with their Creator and Redeemer. What about them?

And to complicate the picture further, I have met popular preachers who are money-hungry, and faith-healers who are unspiritual, and theologians who lack faith and conviction in the very things they are teaching.

All this leaves us with a myriad of questions. Does holiness equate to intimacy with God or with spiritual ministry? Can one be a businessperson or politician and still be holy? Is one holy because one is a priest or monk? Has holiness to do with one's being or one's actions or both?

Now, I do know one 'holy' man whom I greatly admire and respect. But you would probably never pick him out as a 'saint'. He himself would not either, and he would be most embarrassed if he knew I was referring to him. He is not a churchman. He works in the secular world. He is good in his work. He is a person who loves God and cares about other people. He is a man of prayer and humility. He is also a man of vision, courage and faithfulness. And when one is with him, one is edified.

Merton tells us that 'sanctity is not a matter of being less human, but more human...this implies a greater capacity for concern, for suffering, for understanding...and also for humour, for joy'.[15]

Holiness, I believe, is God's grace operating in our lives. It draws us into the life of God and turns us towards the world. Ultimately, holiness has to do with living the will of God by the power and grace of God. The person who lives like this is probably not aware of the fact that he or she is a 'saint'.

Try again

The journey of perseverance

Those living in the First World usually have the expectation that almost anything is possible and that we can have it now. Those from the Third World are not so optimistic or demanding. Subject to long periods of exploitation and oppression, they are less hopeful that things will quickly or easily come their way.

The Western approach to life, when adopted as one's personal lifestyle, is highly problematical. That I can have whatever I want and that things easily fall into my lap is a momentous distortion of reality. It is a modern secular myth that has been raised to the level of unquestionability.

Not only do I disbelieve this myth, my own experience suggests the opposite.

At the age of fourteen my formal education abruptly ended. Being a migrant kid in the Australia of the late 1950s, education was a luxury we could not afford. I had to go to work. But my love of learning and my quest for knowledge did not die at this point. And later, much later, I was able to resume formal education.

In later Christian ministry, I worked for several years as a detached street worker in a decadent inner city area before seeing any fruit on my labours.

And more recently, I finally saw the publication of the first book I wrote some seven years ago. Even though five of my subsequent books had been published, this one was turned down by more publishers than I care to remember. I rewrote it five times.

Merton tells us that 'the thing to do when you have made a mistake is not to give up doing what you were doing and start something altogether new, but to start again'.[16] While this is not absolute advice in that some things need to be abandoned, the challenge to persist is an appropriate one.

Good things may sometimes come easily, but usually they are the fruit of persistent hard work. Quality friendships take time. Honing our skills takes practice. Building community is a long journey.

While tenacity can have its shadow side in that we stubbornly surge forward when in fact we should disengage, to persistently pursue what is worthwhile and good is a quality worth developing.

That compulsive self

Finding a new motivational centre

It must be stated at the outset that not everyone is compulsive. I have friends who are wonderfully easy-going. They focus not so much on the destination, but have a great capacity to enjoy the journey. While they may not be the high achievers of this world, they certainly are warm and wonderful people to be with and to relax with. One friend in particular lives as if he has all the time in the world and all the time for me and others. I like him a lot!

Unfortunately, I am not like that. And that has been sculpted in my early family history. I had to become old when I was still much too young and had to give before I had been adequately given to. This form of deprivation can easily lead to the compulsive self so that one is forever trying to catch what one didn't have in the first place. This is no fun way to live. It's like trying to catch one's tail!

Merton, therefore, rightly reminds us that 'we do not live more fully by doing more, seeing more, tasting more, and experiencing more than we ever have before'.[17]

For a long time, almost blindly, I tried to live contrary to Merton's insight. Part of the difficulty lay in the fact that my motivations were nicely masked by a religious activism.

Evangelical activism expressed in working with problem people, the needy or the poor is quickly, and often mindlessly lauded. Our work with homeless young people and drug addicted youth received not only the blessing of the churches, but also many civic commendations.

And since social problems are never-ending and sometimes ever-increasing, there is always more that can be done. More that should be done!

So I worked hard. Too hard. And I demanded too much of myself and others. I knew how to work, but not to play. The sabbath rhythm of life was conspicuous by its absence. I failed to listen to others and to my own body. The lessons learned in sickness were quickly forgotten in wellness.

In saying all of this, I am not saying that we should not work with zeal, steadfastness and commitment among the poor. Jesus invites us to do so! But our motivations need to be purified. Service needs to be shaped more by the magic of love than by the psychology of our compulsions. And in the long run, it is only love that will fuel us for the long journey of faithful service.

Compulsivity does not die easily. It slowly cracks, however, when we find the grace to face our own pain and loss. It becomes dinted when we are able to journey into emptiness and befriend the empty places of our lives.

The problems of doing too much are not solved by doing less. They are only solved by inner transformations. And these are the work of God's grace. But they require a painful honesty on our part and a preparedness to face the abyss.

While we expect the abyss to be the dark and empty place – and it is that – it is surprisingly also the place where God is found.

Solitude

Stilling the storms within

There is nothing so intrusive and nothing that destabilizes my inner equilibrium as much as emotional pain. And there are no effective pills for inner pain, although we can find ways to suppress these feelings or divert our attention elsewhere. We can also find the courage to face such pain.

Much of my emotional pain has to do with identifying and carrying the pain of those who are particularly dear to me and coping with a sense of loss when dreams and hopes turn out to be so different than expected.

Maybe, others are more inwardly disturbed by other things. Worry and anxiety. Fear. Insecurity. Guilt. These are generally not the 'demons' that plague me. But we all have things that plague our minds and relentlessly disturb our inner sense of peace. And this lack of inner harmony paints everything we are and do, including our relationship with God.

Finding ways to still the storms within is imperative not only for our spirituality, but also for our health, general well-being and effectiveness.

Somewhat foolishly, I used to think that I had to still the storms so that I could come to God in peace and harmony. I usually failed miserably with this approach.

Now I do exactly the opposite. I come to God with my pain. I no longer hide it nor make silly excuses. I open these things to God, awaiting healing, comfort or correction.

Thomas Merton tells us that 'solitude is not something you must hope for in the future. Rather, it is a deepening of the present, and unless you look for it in the present you will never find it.'[18]

If solitude is the experience of stillness and peace in the midst of our daily realities, then it is not necessary that we only find these in the midst of peaceful circumstances and a quiet spirit. The opposite is more frequently the case. Stillness is to be found in the midst of the storm. Peace in the midst of trouble. Comfort in our pain. Quietness in a noisy world.

I know of no better place than to find this stillness in the sheltering and nurturing presence of God who gently embraces me in my pain and brings comfort and encouragement. I, therefore, find stillness not in aloneness, but in the presence of the One who unhesitatingly welcomes me.

A cry for mercy
Acknowledging our own needs

The art of living in our frenetic world has to do with finding ways to be gentle with ourselves. In saying this, I am not talking about being totally self-preoccupied nor condoning of our wrongdoing or mistakes. And I am certainly not suggesting that there are never times when we need to push ourselves to get on with the job.

To be gentle with ourselves does not mean that we are not focused or hard-working. Rather, it has to do with acknowledging our needs and doing something about them.

Thomas Merton rightly points out that 'the man whose prayer is so pure that he never asks God for anything does not know who God is, and he does not know who he is himself for he does not know his own need for God'.[19]

While I find it difficult to imagine that such a person actually exists, it is obvious that he or she lacks both self-awareness and God-awareness and wears the cloak of pharisaical smugness.

That not all of our needs are met is a psychological and existential given. And that we have a profound and deep need of God is a basic tenet of the Christian faith. In fact, our very life is a gift from God and is sustained by God's providence and blessing.

To be gentle with ourselves, therefore, has to do with recognizing our giftedness and our limitations, our tasks and the role that others should play. It involves doing what we must and leaving the rest in God's hand.

But above all, being gentle with ourselves means that we allow others to help, encourage and challenge us and that we acknowledge our need of God's forgiveness, grace and mercy.

Persons who know themselves know their complicity, weakness and sin. And they know their God to whom they can run for help and empowerment.

When things are taken away
Facing life's losses

Life adds things to us. We grow, gain an education, develop skills, become competent. These abilities give us an income and social standing, and maybe even prestige.

Many other, and possibly even more important things are also added. Friendship, family, being a part of certain groups and associations. And hopefully, wisdom and grace and other qualities and virtues are also added to us.

All of the above, for the Christian, may be seen as God's good gifts. For others, they may simply be the result of hard work and self-accomplishment.

But we soon learn that life not only adds things to us, things are also taken away. Certain opportunities are denied us. We diminish in our physical or intellectual powers. We experience sickness and loss. And more tragically, things may be violently taken away from us through physical, emotional or sexual abuse.

So we live in this strange twilight zone of light and darkness. We live a dialectic of having and relinquishment, of holding and withholding.

For most, if not all of us, the experience of loss is difficult. We want to be enhanced, rather than diminished. We want to hold, rather than to let go. And sometimes we desperately try to hang on to things which we should have let go because they have already slipped through our fingers.

The challenge for all of us is to come to terms with loss. For Christians the added challenge is to find God in the midst of our loss.

This may be particularly difficult, especially if we have a theology that is triumphalistic. If we hold the idea that God only gives but does not take away, then in the midst of loss our faith may suffer a severe crisis.

But God does take away! We are invited to experience not only the promised land, but also the desert. We are called to feast and to fast. The gift of life invites us to embrace the gift of death. God lifts us up, but we are also humbled.

Merton notes, one 'cannot rely on structures... they are good and they should help us... but they may be taken away'.[20] And, other things may be taken away as well. To lose a support group, a community of faith or one's vocational community is a great loss, but loved ones or one's health can be lost as well.

What do we do in such situations? There are no easy answers. But loss invites us to the strange journey of surrender and faith. It pulls us into the abyss. It spirals us into circles of pain and maybe self-pity, or despair. It sends us into a dark tunnel where we expect to find nothing and no-one.

But someone can be found, and this may not be the God who rescues. It may simply be the God of the dark day on Golgotha's lonely hill. The God who experienced the greatest loss and who promises companionship in this difficult journey with no end or solution in sight except the promise that this God is also the God of the resurrection, this God may be found when all else is taken away.

Imperfection
The trails of darkness

We all begin that fragile human journey on the basis of care. We are sheltered, nourished and sustained by others, usually our parents.

Over time the journey of care also becomes one of trust. We are no longer simply passive recipients, but actively learn to trust our carers. And for years this trust may continue at the level of great simplicity. It may even continue long after trust should be given.

But sooner or later this delicate fabric is rent as we discover, however haltingly, the realities of imperfection and sometimes more painfully the tragedy of betrayal.

Over time, we discover not only the imperfections of others, but also those of ourselves. And so the battle begins. Do we rationalize? Blame? Defend? Or do we face the music?

And once we begin to wrestle with all of these things, it doesn't take long before we see imperfections writ large everywhere. In our social institutions. The Church. Government. And particularly in the areas of welfare and service to the poor. It is all too evident that we live in a grossly unfair and unjust world.

But I hope that this is not all that you and I see. While this is the total horizon of some people, there is clearly more to our world. There are the archaic trails of innocence. Surprising altruism. Pockets of pristine natural beauty. Creative and comfortable social landscapes. Remnants of neighbourliness. Music and art. The list is endless, for everywhere there are the signs of God's common grace etched on a fragile humanity and an ever more fragile world.

Merton is, therefore, right when he notes that 'all things are at once good and imperfect. The goodness bears witness to the goodness of God, but the imperfection of all things reminds us to leave them [go beyond them] in order to live in hope.'[21]

The marks of God's goodness invite reception, participation, thankfulness and celebration. The reality of imperfection calls us, not to passive resignation, but to an active participation in the difficult journey of transformation.

Imperfection in ourselves, in others and in our world, while it is the ugly stain that mars the beautiful bolt of cloth, and therefore stains no matter how good our washing detergents, does not mean that the cloth should be thrown away, nor that it is now totally useless. Imperfection is so often the genesis of human ingenuity.

In Christian thinking, imperfection is also not the end of the story. It is simply a midpoint. For the story begins with the, oh, so good world that God has made. And it ends with new heavens and a new earth.

Imperfection halts us in our proud march to our own future. It diminishes the human impulse to power which so often is not power *for* others, but power *over* others. It puts us in touch with our own vulnerability and brokenness.

In fact, imperfection and its however reluctant acknowledgement provides us with the first hesitant steps towards God. But they are only the first, because in this quest of transcendent connectedness we also need to discover that God has taken giant strides over centuries of history to come towards us.

In this connectedness of embrace, welcome and forgiveness, we begin the journey as the wounded healers, the forgiven saints, who wish to bring God's shalom and grace to others who waveringly are wanting to take those first steps.

Inner quietude

Entering the inner temple

For the past two weeks, I have been at home by myself and away from the busy routine of work. My wife is presently overseas. And since I am a happy introvert, I was looking forward to this time. A time to be still, to reflect, to pray.

Stillness and solitude are not strangers to me. Long ago they became friends, even though I do have somewhat of an ambivalent relationship with them. So I was looking forward to a positive time. In one sense it has been, but not the way I expected.

Thomas Merton writes, 'we can enter into ourselves as into temples of freedom and light'.[22] That is possible, but only if we have come to a deep inner quietude.

Most of us have had those moments when we have been at peace with ourselves, others and our world. Those are the times when one feels alive in a pristine way. There is a glow to being. A magic to being alive. A joy that pulsates through the very fabric of one's being. At such times we can truly say: It is good! And for the Christian, one can celebrate that God is good.

At these times, one senses an inner purity and wholeness. It is as if God's full shalom has come to us.

But for me these have been moments. A harmonious melody in the midst of discord. An infrequent call of the nightingale. These have not been the normal days and months of my life. Nor the rhythm of the past two weeks.

Inner quietude is not something that we can create. We can be by ourselves. Enjoy relaxing music. Be reflective. But our inner world may be more like an untamed beast than a deer that pants for streams of living water.

In the midst of our stillness, we can be very distracted. For we never quite know what may happen when we move to being still. The gift of peace may come our way. Or a troubled roar from the abyss. Or a pain from our wounded past. Or anxious fears regarding an uncertain future. The list may be endless, but the distractions are real.

Yet none of this should surprise or discourage us. Inner quietude only comes as a gift after the storm. A healing after the purging. A grateful acceptance after relinquishment.

I re-experienced some of these matters during these two weeks. But struggles are not without their blessings. If grace is found for our struggles then we are in fact called forward by the very things that we fear may pull us back.

So while we may wish that our inner beings would be temples of freedom and light, we should still enter even though they be stormy seas, whirlpools of pain, boardrooms of debate, confusing journeys and grottoes of uncertainty. For in the midst of all of that, especially when the opposite was expected, we may well be surprised that God will cleanse the temple. And peace comes as the undeserved gift from the God who enters our journeys and surprises us along the way.

An unremarkable source
Seeing the small beginnings

My family of origin faithfully each year went for annual holidays to the banks of the Noosa River in Queensland. While this was a beautiful and idyllic spot, I soon became bored.

At sixteen years of age I finally gained permission from my parents to go on holidays by myself and for the first time spent three weeks in the subtropical rainforests of the Lamington National Park. This world of wonder: of ghostly antarctic beech forests, palm groves, rocky outcrops, misty mountain peaks, crashing waterfalls, exotic bird life, was to become the world to which I was to return again and again. In this world, Tolkien's creative world would readily have found a home.

I remember on one extended stay in the Lamington that I came across the beginnings of the Coomera River. The Coomera is quite some river closer to the coast. But here, high in the mountains, it was so insignificant. A mere crystal clear trickle gurgling its way among moss-covered rocks.

The humble beginnings of the Coomera is a powerful metaphor of so much of life and spirituality. Such small beginnings. So unremarkable. So fragile and insignificant that it doesn't really warrant our careful attention.

And yet, there, in such common vulnerability and ordinariness lie the first strands of a tapestry still to be woven.

The story of an inn, of hay and dung, of a dislocated girl and a troubled Joseph and a mere whimpering child are the first strands of such a tapestry. Many strands have been added since. But every integral strand had similar unremarkable beginnings. Whether a Francis of Assisi, a John Wesley or a Mother Teresa, their fragile beginnings gave no hint of their future significance and successes.

Thomas Merton suggests that 'it is not sufficient to know the source is there – we must go and drink from it'.[23] That is true! But to recognize something as a source of hope and life is already to have received a great gift. For we so easily pass by. We do not see because we are really looking for something quite different.

Our sadly sidetracked consciousness looks for the powerful, not the vulnerable; the king, not the child; the cathedral not a house gathering of those on bended knee and with trembling heart. Our attention is arrested by the corporation, not by a grassroots cooperative.

The first gift, therefore, is the gift of sight. To see the gift of God on a bloody hill is true sight indeed, sculpted by the mystery of faith and nurtured in the womb of hope. So stark, so ugly and, oh, so wrong. And yet, the mystery of the death of the One as life for so many and those yet to come.

And yes, of course, seeing must move to embracing. We need to embrace the vulnerability of our own prayers and our acts of service and not become dismayed by their seeming insignificance. It is God who adds to our weakness, strength. To our faith, courage. To our smallness, beauty. To the small seed, an abundant harvest.

So let's not be afraid to worship the God of such small things who is also the creator of all.

Being loved
Discovering myself in the face of the Other

Coming to peace with oneself is not the product of a profound self-introspection and self-preoccupation. Nor does a sense of acceptance come via the tortuous route of seeking to gain the approval of parents, or spouse or colleagues.

During several decades of my adulthood I sought to gain the approval of my father who had been absent, through no fault of his, during my early childhood years. I failed miserably in this demanding quest. Not only was I different from my Dad, but I also held very different values. His was the Protestant work ethic of the self-made and independent man. Mine was the journey of faith in serving the poor within the context of Christian intentional community.

This hopeless quest to gain approval did not succeed through greater activity but through abandoning the quest and embracing the gift of the support and encouragement of other older men. Their friendship brought healing to my wounded inner child.

And it is precisely at this point that the mystery of healing and growth lies. When we think we have to do more in order to be accepted and be at peace, we discover that the genius of life lies not in striving, but in receiving. Thomas Merton once noted: 'my true meaning and worth are shown to me not in my estimate of myself, but in the eyes of the one who loves me'.[24] To which we may add: nor is my worth revealed to me in my productivity and achievements.

The one who ultimately looks upon us with the eyes of love, favour and acceptance is the God revealed in the face of Jesus Christ. This God neither abandons, nor ignores, nor rejects us in our failure and folly. Instead, this God draws upon himself the cloak of our shame and inwardly carries the pain of our sin. And instead of then castigating us for our stupidities we are embraced, healed and forgiven.

We are blessed indeed when not only God whom we cannot see but can only know by his Word and Spirit, but also others can mirror this acceptance to us. I have been so blessed. Throughout most of my adult life, older adults have taken a loving and supportive and also challenging interest in me. A seminary professor. A ministerial colleague. A university associate. And many more.

The gift that these people brought was not so much the gift of expertise. It certainly was not the attempt to control. Nor was it primarily the gift of helpfulness. The issue was not what they *did* for me. It was rather that they were there *for* me. Their gift was the gift of companionship. Their blessing was the love which was so undeservedly given.

We know ourselves the best not through archaeological introspection, but in the face of the Other who loves, challenges and affirms. This opens the windows of our life. It makes us soar when we can only think of crawling. It makes us give when we thought we had nothing left to give.

The ongoing journey
Life as unfolding grace

We experience life as a set of constraints as well as a series of opportunities. There is both the givenness of our genetic inheritance and the blessing of creativity. There are the limitations of our circumstances as well as the surprises of the unexpected. There is the work of our own hands as well as the gifts of God's grace.

As a result, there is nothing static about our life. This is not to suggest that there are no regularities or patterns. Nor does it deny that repetition is an important part of our lives. But it does mean that the past does not have the last word. And that while we have to embrace being, we also may celebrate becoming.

Thomas Merton has this to say: 'I am not perplexed either by what I am or what I am not, but by the mode in which I am tending to become what I really will be.'[25] While I am not all that sure that I can share the certainty of the first part of Merton's assertion, I do understand and agree with the last part. What we are becoming is certainly not due to our careful planning.

My life has continued to take surprising turns. I had no idea that I would move from the printing and publishing industry into social welfare. And I never thought that I would move from the work of urban mission into tertiary education. Nor did I ever think when I was madly playing soccer that I would ever write poetry. The surprises are endless.

But what is most surprising of all is not the changes and the different fields of work, but rather that the situations and circumstances which seemed problematical and difficult turned out to be the moments of grace and transformation. Thus Merton is right, we do not really know what God can use to make us into what we are becoming.

A sudden closed door to overseas mission work opened the way to inner-city urban ministry. Working with broken people opened the way to connecting with my own woundedness. Letting go of the joyful experience of working in Asia opened other avenues for service. Sickness helped to make me more radical. Deprivation made me appreciate the plight of the poor. The list is endless. But the point is clear. In the skilful hands of the Creator, chaos turns into the harmony of the created order. In the loving hands of the Redeemer, the wounded places become springs of sustenance and nourishment. In the enlivening energies of the Spirit, creativity comes out of the places of failure and shame.

So while we plan and work and live our life in a challenging world, there are the surprises that shape our minds and hearts and empower our hands. Thus we are called to acknowledge the past, face the present and live unto the future.

BEING AND TRANSCENDENCE
The Search for Ultimate Meaning

There is something most curious about us humans. The mark of creatureliness is stamped upon our very being, and yet we lean towards infinity. The marks of death are finely sketched upon our delicate beginnings and yet we search for life's plenitude and continuity.

This impulse beyond resignation and a dour passivity and fatalism is everywhere writ large on the human story. Philosophy, art, music, the pouring forth of cultural creations and the incessant movement of shaping our world and our landscape all speak of a creativity that longs for the ultimate.

This of course is not to suggest that this is all there is to the human story. There is the abuse of power. Monstrous idolatries. False ideologies. Economic exploitation and oppression. And there are the shameful divisions that mar the practice of justice and equality.

While the above looks more at the macro-level, at the micro-level there are the dysfunctionalities and betrayals that rend apart our personal relationships and our social fabric. The cost of the commitment to an individualism that has no sense of the common good and to a productivity that has lost the ethics of personalism, has been enormous in its bitter harvest.

The tension between our higher aspirations and our shameful abuse and neglect signal the conflict that lies at the heart of the human condition. This tension can finally be traced to the fact that we were created to do God's good in our world, but decided to do our own ambivalent work. This ambivalence is due to the continuing marks of God's grace upon the human community and the persistence of our human autonomy in going our own way.

Merton acknowledges that there is much good in the world. Humans are made in the image of God and therefore their final destiny is to be with God and to live in and for him. But he testifies to our need for God's redemptive and restorative activity. He invites us to the redemptive work of Christ, the renewing work of the Spirit, the unction of baptism, the empowering feast of the eucharist and the sustaining grace of Christian community.

He invites us to the revelation of God's grace, to the following of Jesus, to the practice of love, to the path of peacemaking and to an asceticism that makes room for God in our lives and in our world.

While God's grace has often been cast in the framework that denies the body and magnifies the soul, that rejects the world and longs for heaven, that prioritizes the Church over the human community, it is nevertheless true that a redemption that does not deeply love the neighbour as well as God is a mere distortion of biblical Christianity.

The power of the biblical story lies in a transcendence embodied in the incarnation. God becomes one with us in Christ. And this amazing identification becomes the grace of substitution. God the sinless One takes to himself our sin and shame and frees us to become daughters and sons in the Spirit.

While the Church is called to be a sign and symbol of this amazing transformative activity of the grace of God, the Church cannot hold or contain the action of God. The signs of God's presence are everywhere. The Spirit is at work in the world with revelatory gentleness. And everywhere – in the places of hope and despair – the call to enter the reign of God can be heard.

Whether we come running or we come stumbling, whether we are ready or unprepared, God's grace is there to surprise, renew and empower us.

The challenge, however, is not only to begin this journey, but also to continue the path of renewal and empowerment. It is one thing to come to faith, it is another to grow in faith. It is one thing to believe in Christ, it is another to be conformed to his passion and suffering. It is one thing to begin in the disciplines of the spiritual life, it is another to negotiate the doubts and the dark night of the soul.

There is nothing easy or self-evident about the journey of faith. It knows the gift of peace, but cries for mercy. It knows the blessing of homecoming, but reaches out for a deeper participation in the reign of God.

Transformation
The surprising renewing work of the Spirit

We usually have little idea regarding how it all begins. The awakening of faith is shrouded in as much mystery as the beginnings of the universe. And our many and varied explanations of the work of the Spirit, in renewing us and making us more deeply aware of God's grace, are both helpful and frustrating. Since there is nothing stylized about the work of the Spirit, every typification breaks down under the sheer weight of creativity and surprise.

Thomas Merton gives us one explanatory paradigm: 'one desires to begin a new life because the burden of the old has now become an unbearable accumulation of fatigue, mistakes, betrayals, evasions, disappointments'.[26] This was certainly true of Merton. His life was beginning to run on empty and was lubricated with the oil of despair. Moreover, his life's direction had become a series of side eddies.

People come to faith on similar grounds to Merton. Life has lost its sheen. One's hopes and dreams are in disarray. Obstacles, seemingly impossible to overcome, are strewn on one's pathway. Difficulties mar the texture of our lives. And internally the questions of hope, peace and forgiveness cry out for answers in the face of despair, turmoil and guilt. To such, the Spirit brings the light of God's forgiveness and embrace and healing that bring hope and peace.

Others do not experience the grace of God in quite the same way. As a teenager coming to faith in Christ my life felt far from an unbearable accumulation of fatigue, mistakes and betrayals. I was energetic and hopeful, but lacked an authentic experience of God's nurturing presence. As a result, I was inwardly lost though outwardly successful. For me, the Spirit's work was in making Jesus believable and God present.

For others, the story of transformation may be different again. Some come to faith like the gradual dawning of a new day. Others, through tragedy and the imminent presence of death, find hope in the God of Abraham, Isaac and Jacob.

Others are taken completely by surprise. Life is good and trouble and tragedy are far from the doors of their dwelling. There are no internal struggles and the deeper questions of life's purpose are not even entertained. But the Spirit strikes with revelatory power, opening up a vision of God, the need for repentance, and the challenge to embrace God's grace in Christ.

What is important here is not the many possible ways in which the Spirit may do its renewing work, but that God's Spirit is at work in our world and in our lives. How amazing that the creator of this universe should concern himself with us! How incredible that God's love should reach out towards us and draw us into God's embrace! And how incredible is the particularity of the way this occurs in each of our lives!

If the beginnings of our experience of the grace of God are full of surprises, then surely the secret of Christian life is to remain open to the ongoing mystery of God's work in our lives. While liturgy, theology and Christian community all contribute to structure and stabilize the Christian experience, we need the renewing breath of God's Spirit to push the boundaries, to open new vistas, and to empower us for love and service.

God's benediction
Grace from an irresistible Lover

Thomas Merton makes the assertion that a monk is someone 'kissed by God'.[27]

I am quite sure that Merton does not believe that only monks are so blessed because of their commitment to celibacy, poverty and obedience. Nor that their life of worship, prayer, silence, community and work, in and of itself, invites God's special benediction.

To be kissed by God does not suggest a relationship of work and rewards. It hints at something quite different. It is much more the relationship of love, friendship, closeness, spontaneity and joy.

This kind of relationship is clearly not the sole domain of the professional religious, be they monk, priest, clergyperson or missionary. In fact, in some ways, these may be the last candidates for such a relationship. The more religious life is professionalized, the more it can become a part of one's social and public persona while the heart may remain detached, cold or even indifferent.

The professional religious has no inside edge to the walk of faith, the life of prayer, the search for spirituality, the struggles of obedience. They have no shortcut to the heart of God, let alone to God's special blessings.

The irony of God lies precisely in the strange way that God draws near to people and touches them with the magic of an other reality. And when we make Scripture our guide, we discover that the most obvious candidates are so often overlooked. Jacob, rather than Esau. The Hebrews, rather than any of the other powerful nations of that time. The harlots and prostitutes, rather than the religious of Jesus' day. Galilean fisherfolk, rather than the intelligentsia of Jerusalem.

The Bible's bizarre genealogy is a list reflecting the inclusive nature of God's grace and the welcome of the unlikely.

I also know the kiss of God, but not because I am a religious professional. I experienced it long before I taught theology.

The first was the kiss of embrace and welcome. I remember well the many years of the lonely, seeking heart even though I lived in the religious world of regular church-going. So close, and yet so far from the heart of God. The search seemed to be endless, the finding impossible, and yet the embrace of God came so simply, so powerfully, so transformatively.

However, one can't really sustain an intimate relationship on the basis of one kiss. And that is not how God chooses to interact with us, particularly not in the long journey of faith. There the kisses of healing, comfort and encouragement are needed and freely given to those who remain open to the surprise rather than the predictability of God.

All of this is not to say that God is simply a blind but generous lover who knows nothing of responsibility, obedience, commitment and service. Of course not!! But that God is the irresistible lover is without doubt. And that we are invited to imbibe that love and ladle it out in generous quantities, is without doubt a mark of those who know the kiss of God.

Presence
Experiencing God in everyday life

There is nothing quite so uplifting and encouraging as to experience God's unseen presence. This usually manifests itself in a peace and a sense of God's sheltering nearness.

While we may experience this in times of corporate worship or personal prayer and reflection, God also draws close in the ordinary ebb and flow of life. Relaxing at home, in the pressured workplace, in the joy of friendship and in the challenges of study, God can be as present to us as in the sanctuary or the place of prayer.

In the quiet place we can be more attentive to God's presence. It becomes the time for refreshment and direction. There we can experience healing and encouragement for the journey of life and new direction as we orient our life to knowing and doing the will of God. But in the rugged realities of everyday life, God's Spirit can also be present and give courage, hope, strength, wisdom and peace.

What I am saying is that the whole of life may be lived in God's presence, and the realization of this blessing has as much to do with God's good pleasure as with our own prayerfulness, openness and humility.

Yet God's seeming absence is also a part of our experience. Merton writes, 'one day I woke up to find out that the peace I had known for six months or more had suddenly gone'.[28]

I have had similar unsettling experiences. The most devastating came many months after my dramatic conversion. God's cradling love disappeared as surely as sunshine in a summer's storm. Other experiences of God's absence have hounded my spiritual journey. And while some of these were due to my sin and disobedience, other experiences remain puzzling even to this day.

Since we cannot make sense of everything that happens, resignation to mystery is one option. But I sometimes wonder whether absence is simply a different form of presence. We can be away from a friend and yet be very close, perhaps even closer. Similarly, God may seem very far away and the heavens as brass, yet God is still protecting and sustaining our life.

In the presence of God's absence lie valuable experiences for our spiritual growth and development. Not the least, is learning to trust

God irrespective of whether we experience God's consolation or desolation. Equally important, we need to learn and relearn not to make experience the foundation of our faith, but instead rely on God's promises. But finally, in the emptiness of absence we will struggle, pray and wait till God's face once again shines upon us.

The ongoing journey
Welcoming lifelong conversion

There are some who want to cast all spiritual experiences in rosy terms. So they speak of light, warmth, peace and blessing.

While these sorts of experiences are clearly a part of the story, there is more. And the more also needs to be told lest we fall into an anorexic storytelling that distorts the spiritual journey.

Spiritual experience can also be full of anguish since this not only adds things to our life, but also takes away and transforms the core of who we are.

There is a certain violence in the spiritual quest since God comes to us as both the giver, but also as the great disturber. The Spirit comes to renew and transform, not simply to give another coat of paint. And this activity is neither pleasant nor painless!

Merton speaks of the work of God in our lives as a series of inner revolutions. He goes on to comment: 'While we may have the generosity to undergo one or two such upheavals, we [often] cannot face the necessity of further and greater rendings of our inner self.'[29]

I appreciate what he is suggesting, for I have struggled with the ongoing changes that the spiritual journey demands.

While my conversion to Christ was a life-giving and unburdening experience, the presence of God's light brings with it an exposure of darkness. And I soon realized that following Christ involved making many more changes in my life than I had first anticipated.

Receiving the life of Christ involves being bound to him and to his values and concerns. And obedience to Christ meant that Christ could point my life in a very different direction – which he did!!

Within several years I found myself outside of the familiar and secure world of printing and publishing and in the risky world of working in Aboriginal communities in inland Western Australia.

Nothing has been predictable since. And what on the surface looked like a good spiritual step to take, frequently turned out to be full of difficulty as well.

I remember being part of a small theological student prayer group where for many years we prayed that we would be able to live and serve God more fully in the power of the Spirit. A good step to take without doubt! But the consequences of spiritual renewal brought trouble with the Church and unexpected suffering as well as many blessings and great joy and new energies.

And so it is not surprising that after several such experiences of upheaval and change, one wants to settle down. No more challenges for me, thank you, God!

But this is not how the journey is scripted. Christ continues to call us to walk the narrow road and the unfamiliar path.

At the heart of this journey, Christ calls us into fellowship with his sufferings. We are called to downward mobility, to relinquishment, to servanthood. We are challenged again to let go of our way and to walk the strange journey of faith. In this, while seeming to lose our life, we in fact gain life in abundance and joy.

A prayer of the heart
Identifying what we most desire

I used to think that a prayer of the heart was simply a heartfelt prayer – a prayer of sincerity. But for the writers on Christian spirituality, it has a much deeper meaning. While I intellectually accepted this fuller meaning later in my life, sincerely practising this form of prayer came much later still. Thomas Merton gives us his prayer of heart: 'let my eyes see nothing in the world but your glory, let my hands touch nothing that is not for your service'.[30] A beautiful, if not a seemingly impossible prayer, for in our broken world we so seldom see the glory of God, and so much that we do is service for ourselves rather than acts of praise to the God we adore.

For several years I have prayed: Lord fill me with your light and give me healing hands. An equally strange and impossible prayer perhaps, and worse, a somewhat disjointed prayer. It is certainly a prayer that lacks literary finesse!

My desire was not so much to have a healing ministry where people were helped with overcoming their physical problems. It was much more a desire to be used by God to bring help, encouragement and restoration to people and to the communities of faith to which they belonged. And I believed that for this to occur an ongoing transformation would have to take place in my own life. Hence, my prayer: fill me with your light!

There is nothing terribly sophisticated about my prayer. Merton's is much better. But that is not the point. The prayer of heart is what you truly desire for the sake of the kingdom of God. It is the prayer you carry with you every day for a period of time, sometimes for several years and maybe all your life. It is the prayer you are praying even when you are not praying. It is there in the depths of your being. It is a desire you breathe, eat and sleep.

In one sense, the prayer of the heart is not your prayer, or mine. It is put there by the grace and Spirit of God. But it has found a lodging place within the heart. It resonates in the depths of one's being.

The prayer of the heart is a prayer beyond our own concerns. It is one that seeks God's glory and as such it is prayer that never comes to fulfilment, for our ability to bring glory to God will always be incomplete. Nevertheless, this prayer will set us in a particular direction with many blessings and groanings along the way.

Inner stillness

Creating the free places

In one sense, I am not a good person to write about this topic. Disengagement, inner quietude, rest, peace are more the surprises of my life rather than a deep and abiding reality. I am more steeped in the Protestant work ethic, without, rather than with, a true experience of sabbath.

But I am learning. And life's greatest challenges require grace and perseverance.

Thomas Merton makes the bold assertion that 'without the night spirit, the dawn breath, silence, passivity, man's nature cannot be itself'.[31]

This first of all has to do with entering the cycles of God's created order. Cycles of night and day, planting and harvesting, activity and rest. Cycles which have become partly distorted the more we live the urban reality.

But it also has to do with entering the cycles of God's redemptive activity and grace. To be blessed with a good night's sleep is wonderful. But of itself this is not enough. To be physically refreshed is important, but to be emotionally and spiritually renewed is also very important. In fact, it is foundational and may well be the basis for a peaceful sleep.

Entering into the cycle of God's redemptive activity is first of all the invitation to come home to the heart and presence of God. It is the call to stop wandering. The whisper to disengage. The challenge to turn around. It flags that we cease to rely only on ourselves, and learn to place the big issues of our lives in the hands and direction of God.

But there is more to this redemptive rhythm than the call to surrender. There is also the gentle but persistent reminder to be with this God who has called us. This has to do with fellowship, presence, being attentive to.

In our inner crowded lives and not escaping our outer crowded urban landscape, we cannot be attentive to anything unless we make room, disengage from our many other activities and learn to be still so that we can become present to ourselves and to our God.

Both are necessary. We can't be fully present to God if we are not present to ourselves, for then we only bring to God the social persona or the fragments of our lives or the immediate and pressing issues. But God invites us to bring our whole selves: our daily activities, but also our inner aspirations and dreams.

On the other hand, to attempt to be fully present to ourselves without the presence of God is equally undesirable. For we may well plunge into darkness with no light. Probe questions with no answers. But more seriously, we can't know ourselves unless we do so in the mirror of God's love.

All of this suggests that we need to make room in our lives. Like Bethlehem at the time of the census, our lives are too crowded. There is no room for the Christchild, nor for the Trinity to make their dwelling among us.

The art of uncrowding is the seedbed for the spiritual journey. The night to worship and rest. The early morning to pray and prepare. The day to work but also to disengage to be with the God who journeys with us in all that we do.

Interiority

Building our inner life

In the earlier days of my spiritual journey I would not have been able to make a lot of sense of the idea of building an inner life. The community of faith to which I belonged placed a much higher value on preaching rather than prayer and on the shaping of a Christian mind rather than the development of certain spiritual disciplines. In this church tradition anything to do with the practice of silence or meditation was seen as indulging in subjectivism and moving towards mysticism.

While these concerns may be valid in that we can become too subjectively focused and too inward so that we lose a passionate concern for the pains of the world, we do need to build an inner life. This is not at all to suggest that we build it through our own resources. That is not possible. Such a life can only be built by the grace of God, the wisdom of God and the Spirit of God. But we also play a part.

Merton sometime after his conversion makes the confession, 'I had an interior life, real, but feeble and precarious.'[32] This is not to say that the grace of God was ineffective in his life. It is simply admitting that the practice of prayer, reflection, being still before God, listening and obedient to the promptings of the Spirit were underdeveloped and difficult for him.

It is appropriate for me to make a similar confession, but possibly for different reasons. My coming to faith took on an activist orientation. I felt the need to change the world. Consequently, my prayer life was mainly outwardly focused. Prayer had to do with ministry. I had little understanding of my need for the sheltering and nurturing presence of God.

Today, several decades later, I am still an activist. But the issue of building an interior life has not only become more pressing, but also more desirable. I want to be with God, not simply I want God to bless my ministry. As a result, I have made the spaces in my life to come to silence, to reflect and meditate, to pray, to listen.

I still feel that I am merely a beginner. But I am not only more convinced of how much I need God in my life, I am excited to be in a place of communion, presence and connectedness, the place of God's gentleness and power.

Surprised by the Spirit

God's renewing gift

I was brought up in a church tradition where reference to the Spirit always ran a bad third. Mainly, the Spirit wasn't even in the race!

The Spirit appeared to be some dangerous factor that was supposed to lead to emotionalism and mysticism. And since the knowledge of God had to be a rational affair, and the worship of God a subdued affair, and the Christian life a sober affair, the strange wind of the Spirit hardly caused a flutter in the solemn assembly.

Thankfully this is not the end of the story. It seldom is!

While forms of Christianity may carry a certain cultural stamp, this is hardly the end of the matter.

A dour Dutchman would hardly worship God in the same way as

an emotive Latino. But even the former can be made to dance in the power of the Spirit!

But openness to the surprise of the Spirit seldom comes when we are safe, settled and satisfied with our religious structures and experiences. Instead, it seems that when the smooth flow of tradition is suddenly ruptured, or when we are in the midst of a crisis or in unfamiliar emotional territory, we are strategically placed to be open to the new.

Thomas Merton notes that 'from the abyss there comes, unaccountably, the mysterious gift of the Spirit sent by God to make all things new'.[33]

This is the amazing surprise. When the old answers are no longer satisfying, when old programs are no longer life-giving and when present difficulty and distress crowd in upon us, we expect that things may well fall apart. We fear abandonment and expect despair. And while the pit may be deeper than we had anticipated, we can experience the strong grip of God and the wind of the Spirit carrying us to new realms of faith, hope and trust.

I can well remember a period where my head was full of theology, but my heart was estranged from the affections of God. A time where the slow cancer of rationalism had all but destroyed any openness to mystery and the strange but renewing powers of the Spirit. Yet it was precisely in this dark and empty place that new life sprang forth.

That some of these dark places also become the places of prayer is hardly surprising. But the renewing Spirit comes not only when we are seeking and attentive, but also when we are all but asleep. At such times the surprise is all the greater.

While the Spirit may need to come with a purging presence, it is the life-giving and renewing work of the Spirit that propels us out of the dark places. Or rather, the dark places that are still with us become transformed so that instead of binding us with the bands of despair they become the seedbeds of hope and new action.

The ascetic dimension
When giving away is a good thing

In our contemporary religious world many are the voices that trumpet the gospel of fullness. Fed by the narcissism of our culture, this gospel knows only the message of fulfilment. God's blessings are given to make us better, whole, integrated and empowered.

Clearly, there is much here that is true. God's grace in Christ is given to bring us fullness of life.

But, this is one-sided. It is like looking at the sunlight and forgetting the shadows. It is like the storyteller who recounts his or her life and celebrates all the good and the fun, but skips over the broken dreams, the disappointments and the heartaches.

There is a flipside to the gospel of fullness. It is the gospel of emptiness. God gives, but also takes away. No resurrection is possible without the prior journey into the bowels of death.

Just as the spiritual life can't flourish without the smile of God's shalom, so it can't mature without the dark night of the soul. The bounteous muchness of God's grace is to find its counterpoint in the blight of the desert wind.

This rhythm of life should not simply be circumstantial in that life has its light and shadows. Nor should we only wait for God's double dealing in our lives when we receive both affirmation and correction. This rhythm can also be a self-conscious choice. What I mean by that is that we may build an ascetic dimension to our lives where we structure for emptiness and not only fullness.

Thomas Merton out of his experience as a Trappist monk makes the observation that 'no contemplative life is possible without ascetic self-discipline'.[34] But this is true for all on the spiritual journey. However, to build such disciplines into the lives of those who live out their vocation in normal life, is a particular challenge.

Over the years, I have made many attempts, but with varying success. In fact, the stop–start of so many disciplines and projects became wearisome and discouraging.

A number of things, however, have worked reasonably well. The one is withdrawal by having prayer walks and times of silence within the pattern of my normal day. This is very doable, particularly for an introvert.

What is far more challenging is to develop ascetic practices which run opposite to our core behaviours. If greed lies dormant yet active at the centre of my being, then the practice of various forms of self-denial is appropriate.

None of all of this, and the various ways different forms of asceticism may take, has anything to do with gaining God's credit. We live out of God's grace. But it does have everything to do with developing a spiritual attentiveness.

If we are too full, there is no room for the surprises which come out of creating the spaces for solitude. Asceticism in itself does not make us holy, it merely unclutters us. And those with empty hands will be filled.

Gratitude

Living out of a joyful centre

Every so often I literally pinch myself in sheer amazement regarding the way life has turned out for me. Some might say that I have been greatly blessed. And yet I have no idea why.

I certainly do not believe that blessings have come my way because I have some inside edge on the generosity of God or because I have done amazing things which have won God's favour. I don't believe that we can impress God in that sort of way. And I don't have a repertoire of great deeds!

Moreover, I have friends in the faith in the First World whose love and commitment to God have been exemplary and yet life for them has been one series of trials after another. And my friends in the Third World, despite their fervent faith, virtues and hard work, continue to live in poverty. This also I do not fully understand.

So I live with the mystery of God's great generosity towards me, while I live with the pain of seeing those I deeply care about suffer and struggle so much. And I am caught. I can't remove their struggles and pain, no matter how much I may want to. And I can't and should not negate the graciousness of God towards me.

Merton makes the observation that 'unless we are grateful for our own existence, we do not know who we are, and we have not yet discovered what it really means to be and to live'.[35]

The point that is being made is that life can only truly be lived out of a deep sense of gratitude. So much has been given: life, nurture, training, giftedness, capacity, faith, hope, love. The list is endless! And the basis for rejoicing is great!

So why do I feel so blessed? Is it because I am rich or have power or fame? Certainly not! Is it because I have achieved everything that I have ever wanted? Of course not! And is it because I have never experienced trials and difficulties? Who hasn't? These things are part of the very fabric of our ambivalent and fragile existence!

My deep sense of gratitude springs from the wonder that in the midst of a world so full of unfaith, God has been kind enough to stoop down into my tiny world. I marvel that in the midst of my stumbled searching, God has made himself present to me.

And despite experiences of the dark night of the soul, doubt, and the angry questions that I have hurled at God particularly in the light of his seeming powerlessness in a world that is unjust, God has continued to undergird my very existence.

I see all that has been given not as coming from my own efforts and achievements, but as gifts from the bounteous hand of God. So often, I have received even when nothing was expected. Especially when nothing was expected!

But this sense of gratitude does not leave me footloose and fancy free. I am under a joyful obligation: to live the freedom of God's generosity which makes me the servant of God and neighbour.

Gratitude is the true posture of our relationship to God and to others. Gratitude helps us to see life as a gift. It evokes celebration. And it empowers us for service.

A life of gratitude is fuelled by a magic that helps us to walk the long journey up hills and down dales. Peaks and the deepest abyss cannot stop the one who lives gratefully out of the presence of God.

Providence

The little surprises in an often silent universe

In all honesty, I would have to admit that I have experienced as much of the absence of God as God's presence. This is not to say that God's absence has always been a troubling experience. God's absence has not meant abandonment, and the lack of God's presence has always given me a hunger to seek for renewal and intimacy.

I have deliberately not said that the experience of God's absence has always led me to repentance. I believe that sin is not always the problem. Sometimes, God withdraws because we have to learn lessons of faith and trust when we are in the desert instead of in the paradise of our spiritual experiences.

At the same time, I am happy to report of the many times when God was close not only in personal prayer or in corporate worship, but also in the many incidents and blessings that have come my way through God's providential goodness.

We all have stories that bring encouragement and hope and speak of God's providential care. Merton tells of reading the right book at the right time: 'there are times when ten pages of some book fall under your eye just at the moment when your life, it seems, depends on your reading those ten pages'.[36]

I can multiply such stories from my own experience, and you have yours as well. People coming into our lives at the moment we needed their input and help. An unexpected word of encouragement from an unlikely source. Someone's practical help at a time of crisis.

One of my more bizarre experiences was walking along a lonely beach on a virtually deserted island praying for a small amount of money for transport to get me off the island and I had the appropriate dollar bill wash onto the sand where I was walking.

While the sceptic may explain these strange interventions as chance or coincidence, the Christian interprets them as signs of God's providential care. And the thought that God could be involved in the nitty-gritty details of our lives is comforting and encouraging.

However, none of this means that we can order our lives as if God will always do such things. That would make for a belief in magic and would undermine a life of responsibility. But that God continues to surprise us in the most unexpected ways can and should be a part of the life of faith.

Mysticism
Looking for light and life

My early religious tradition knew nothing of asceticism and mysticism. These were seen as unnecessary and even dangerous. Asceticism was seen as irrelevant because of Christ's finished work on the cross. No acts of sacrifice could add anything to what Christ had done in gaining redemption for us. And mysticism was seen as undermining the clarity of God's revelation. This was seen as erring in favour of the Spirit rather than emphasizing the power of the Word.

The emphasis in this religious tradition, therefore, was on living out of the benefits of the work of Christ and embracing a reasonable faith.

There is much that I still appreciate about this tradition, and I continue to live out of its insights and richness.

But I have never been fully comfortable. I have often wondered whether the Dutch Reformed faith has arisen from the austerity and economy common to the Northern European mind-set. That it is a faith shaped by the pragmatism of a small land that has ever battled the power of awesome seas on its fragile shores and dykes. And that the business rationality of the Dutch also found inroads into the way it understood and shaped the Christian faith.

And of course, I often wondered why a Latino faith, for example, was so very different with its emphasis on imagery, emotive piety and celebration.

It didn't take all that long to come to the realization that faith, worship, prayer are also shaped by the cultural contexts in which they emerge and come to expression.

And so I became a pilgrim. I wandered to faraway lands. But

more importantly, I began to wander in the inner world. Not that I thought that I could discover something there that was not evident in Scripture. But I felt that touching the inner world had something to do with understanding the mystery of the God who makes himself known not only in the great acts of history and in the fragility of the communities of faith, but also in the questions and emptiness of the human heart.

That journey has barely begun, even though it is already many years old. It has called for various forms of asceticism: the voluntary saying of 'no' to the good things of life in order to create space and become more attentive to the Spirit of God and the quests of my inner being. I have not made this journey alone, but am listening carefully to the long tradition of Christian spirituality with its many signposts.

At the heart of this quest lies the key to the Carmelite tradition which, in the words of Thomas Merton, 'teaches above all ... the way of the hidden life'.[37] The life that knows detachment in order to more deeply draw near to the heart of God. That knows emptiness not in order to be filled, but to know God more fully.

This mystical journey has nothing to do with an escapism from the stark realities of life. I live in the midst of them, especially since I live with the poor. Mysticism is the journey of faith in the light of the mystery of the weakness of God who seeks to empower the poor.

The inner quest can never be simply for its own sake. It is for God and the neighbour. It is seeking the heart of God which beats for a world in pain and travail.

Prayer walks
Developing disciplines of spirituality

We begin the Christian journey by utilizing the disciplines of the Christian life provided by the community of faith to which we belong. And from the benefits of these, our hesitant footsteps are guided on the road to spiritual growth and maturity.

Initially, we may be unaware that this may constitute a domestication of the more innocent and spontaneous ways in which we seek to express our friendship relationship with the Triune God. I remember only too well how quickly street young people with no previous church background moved from their delightful ways of praying with its refreshing non-use of churchy in-talk, to praying like the rest of us!

As we begin this amazing journey of faith, we may also be unaware that different Christian religious traditions emphasize different themes and promote different strategies in the spiritual quest. Some major on sacrament, others on word, others again on prayer. Some emphasize the Spirit, others service. Some make much of worship, others the importance of silence and meditation.

In time, we must come to the realization that while we should make use of the strengths of our own Christian tradition, we must look at the particular charisms of other faith communities. So as a Calvinist Christian, I have learnt from the Anabaptists and Pentecostals and Charismatics, and as a Protestant Christian, I have learnt much from Roman Catholics. The task here is not to reduce all of this to a fruit salad. Rather, it is enriching one's own tradition through making use of the strengths of other Christian traditions.

But, finally, while respecting the strengths of one's own faith community and listening to and adapting features of others, one does have to make one's own way in the spiritual journey. This is not an appeal to a rugged Western individualism which negates the role of community, but it does recognize the need for particularity.

Your way of listening to God or your way of praying or meditating may not at all suit me. And somewhere, I need to find the courage to make my own spiritual journey while still listening to the wisdom of others.

Merton tells us: 'I have got in the habit of walking up and down under the trees along the wall of the cemetery in the presence of God.'[38]

I have developed similar and other disciplines.

Regular prayer walks have long been a part of my life. So have sacramental showers at the end of a long day that involved a lot of counselling. A cup of coffee with a friend or colleague can be turned into sharing the Lord's Supper together. The possibilities are endless, but the impact is eternal.

In our technological age, so proud of its progress and often so devoid of tapping the sources for inner nourishment, there is a great need for us to develop spiritual disciplines to remain connected with the God of life.

Moreover, our churches, so much given to rituals and routines and ceremonies, often do not serve us well in the spiritual quest.

The challenge, therefore, is to listen to the long heritage of Christian mysticism and reflection, but more particularly to carve out our own disciplines and establish our own spiritual traditions so we can all continue to be connected and attuned to the God who calls us into renewal and intimacy and into doing his will in our lives and world.

Listening

Opening our inner ear

I enjoy listening to others, particularly when people come for counselling, sharing, mentoring or spiritual direction. I am pretty hopeless at listening to speeches or lectures, unless of course the speaker is particularly captivating. And I am not good at all at listening to what I regard as non-sense or gossip. In fact, I am quite intolerant and have been known to walk out of such conversations.

Because I am highly intuitive, I have also learned to hear what people are not saying and this has been helpful especially in counselling and mentoring.

But I am not at all sure whether I have learned to listen well to God. I find it difficult to come to stillness. I tend to be impatient and frequently run ahead. And often, I have too many ideas of my own. I am sure that God must often feel that I want to give him a bit of a helping hand. I am equally sure that God is not impressed!

Merton reminds us that 'to listen to God means, first of all, to recognise our helplessness, our stupidity, our blindness and our ignorance'.[39]

While careful listening in counselling is for the benefit of the other person, listening to God is for our own. Sadly, we often fail to realize how much we need to hear God's wisdom and learn his ways.

Listening to God involves listening to Scripture, but it has to do with listening to the Bible in a particular way. It is reading Scripture meditatively. It seeks to hear the voice of God in the word of God, a voice that speaks personally, directly and sometimes urgently.

Listening to God also involves hearing God's whispers in the quiet place of solitude and prayer. While listening to Scripture gives us the guidelines by which God wants us to live, in solitude we often hear the more specific things we need to know for our life direction.

This is not to suggest that listening to God is only for wisdom and direction. So often listening is for intimacy, comfort, nurture, shelter and empowerment.

The art of listening is an act of humility. It is admitting that I do not know and don't have the answers. And so we turn to God so that he may shine his light upon us – for it is in God's light that we see light.

In Christ
The miracle of new life

My own journey to faith was an agonizing one. Even though I was brought up in a Christian family and regularly went to church, I was not a person of faith. The opposite was true. I was disillusioned with what I saw of Christianity and my inner life was in turmoil, frequently bordering on despair.

The repetition in my dream life was being on the edge of something that turned into a downward spiralling vortex that landed me in the embrace of the abyss.

Though outwardly calm and functional and even successful in sport and schooling, my inner world was a mess. My overriding sense was one of loneliness and abandonment even in the midst of family and friends. And God, if there was such a reality, was mockingly absent.

And since I was characterized by an arrogance which I wore like the protective armour that it wasn't, I failed to turn to anyone for help. Neither family nor friends, clergy nor counsellors were given a window into my life, let alone into my struggles.

Conversion and coming to faith in Christ was not a mere religious commitment. It was not simply suddenly believing something that I had previously doubted. And it certainly had nothing to do with Christ becoming an addendum to my life.

It was all wonderfully different. It was an embrace. And it was so powerfully yet gently transformative that it has provided the central impulse for the rest of my life.

Merton says it in such a simple yet almost naive way: 'the Christian life is nothing else but Christ living in us by his Holy Spirit'.[40]

I think it should be said very differently, even though the above is true. Becoming a Christian is the most liberating of all of life's experiences, and being a Christian is one of the most exciting adventures one can ever embark on.

Being a Christian is so much more than the repetition of form and creed. It is more than the routines of worship and the disciplines of spirituality. It is the awesome experience of God's presence and the excitement of being a part of God's purposes for our time.

Does this mean that my Christian journey has been a smooth and progressive one? Of course not! It has been very up and down. Full of good things and difficulties. Triumphs and failures.

But the central impulse has remained. The welcoming and empowering grace of God has carried me thus far. So should I doubt now? Or can the adventure continue? Of course it can!

Creating empty spaces
Reorganizing our life for prayer and reflection

While those who are marginalized, and particularly those who are unemployed or the elderly, may experience time differently, most of us are only too aware of how little time we have to do everything we want. Life is the busy round of family, friends, work, church, social responsibilities and recreation, with work often predominating.

Some of us have so much to do that we wish for an eight-day week and long for several lifetimes. Why we have so much to do has something to do with the hectic pace of life, the complexity of our social world, the rush of urban realities. But it also has to do with the frenetic desire to be more and do more. It is fed by our own inner compulsions.

It is obvious that this kind of pace cannot be maintained without cost to our health, family, relationships and our spirituality. In fact, this way of living is a manifestation of an inner destructiveness where we try to do more than what God asks of us. And thus we live life against itself by busily doing and giving while failing to be nurtured and empowered.

Into this madness needs to come the breath of God's gentleness which is best received in the place of prayer and the place of stillness.

Merton reminds us that 'prayer, meditation and contemplation may fill the space created by the abandonment of other concerns'.[41] This may be said a little stronger. It has to be created by letting go of other things, otherwise the quiet place will never come into existence, it will simply remain the busy and frenetic place.

And how do we come to such a quiet place, a place of prayer? Never easily or cheaply! I had to be dragged there by my own needs, my inability to respond to the pain and difficulty in the lives of others, and by the growing realization that I needed to go God's way far more than pursuing my own way.

Today, I do not *have* time for prayer and contemplation. I *make* time. I take hold of opportunities: a cancelled appointment, waiting for someone, walking home, cancelling going to a movie. The opportunities are endless if the desire and the will are present.

The dark night
The journey without signposts

I have some Christian friends who are seemingly always joyful and profoundly positive about everything that is happening to them.

They see the positive side of things, including those I think are pure disasters.

And their faith is always buoyant and upbeat. God is firmly entrenched in his royal heaven and all is well on earth for those who trust him.

I must admit that I admire these friends for their positive outlook on life. But I often wonder whether they are living in reality? Or perhaps bliss can be squeezed out of the gourd of denial?

My own experience is often disappointingly different. I see the dark and negative things as much as the good and the delightful. And my journey of faith has not been without the experience of the dark night of the soul. In fact, several experiences of the dark night have left me wondering whether I am just slow in getting my spiritual act together or whether I was a candidate for a double dosage because of my sombre Calvinist upbringing.

The dark night is no picnic one decides to attend. It finds us, and usually at the strangest junctures of our lives. It occurs at the points of the journey where the underground geophysical plates of our very being are shifting.

Merton reminds us that in the dark night of the soul God deprives people 'of the light and consolation which they seek, by impeding their own efforts, by confusing and depriving them of the satisfactions which their own efforts aim to attain'.[42]

But there may be other ways of understanding this part of the spiritual journey, although understanding may not be the most appropriate term. The dark night is always a mysterious and disturbing reality.

For me, it has been more the move from the God of the exodus to the God of captivity. Or to put that differently, the dark night has made God the present friend into God the absent partner. Or differently again, the God of the familiar signposts becomes the God of unfamiliar desert places.

The impact of this varies, but for this traveller on the road of faith it has caused everything to shake, since God is no mere appendix to my life. Instead, when the central core seems to crumble it takes most things in its sweep.

The secret is to let things fall. And this strikes at the very heart of our need to be in control and self-sufficient. Striking at the heart of a predictability which so easily leads to legalism, we find that in the darkness and chaos a new simplicity and trust is born.

In coming out of the tunnel of the dark night of the soul we never find ourselves in the same room though we are still resident in the house of faith.

Prayer
The Spirit's work within us

There is a double and yet interrelated rhythm of life. The one is our proactive attempt to impact the world around us. This is the process of externalization. We go into the world to shape it and so we promote our programmes and build our institutions. The other is receptive rather than outgoing. Here, we receive the good things that life offers us. Here, we are the beneficiaries of the many undeserved blessings that come our way.

The disciplines of the spiritual life operate in a similar way. This is especially true of the gentle art of prayer.

We not only come to prayer. Prayer also comes to us. Sadly, we so often know only the former and neglect the latter.

Much of our praying is essentially activist. We have our valid concerns and our pressing needs and we are busy telling God about these things and asking him to do something about them. Usually we are, and we expect God to be, in express delivery mode.

There are other ways of being activist in prayer. There are the needs of others and the concerns for our world. We pray prayers of intercession, deliverance and healing.

But there are also other forms of prayer. We not only engage in prayer, prayer also engages us.

Merton reminds us that 'deep interior prayer comes to us . . . at work, in the middle of our daily business, at a meal, on a silent road, or in a busy thoroughfare'.[43]

These are the prayers that we have not planned or anticipated.

They emerge out of the deep inner recesses of our own being or come from the gentle yet persistent nudges of the Spirit.

While the other forms of prayer are deliberate and focused, these prayers are the interruption and the surprise. And they may well be some of the most important prayers that we pray.

These prayers may well put us in touch with what is more basic to our very existence. And they may put us in touch with the heart of God and his concerns.

The challenge for us is to recognize these gentle nudges when they come our way and to make these our urgent and important prayers.

When our heart is towards God then the whispers of his Spirit will certainly come our way.

Willing renunciation
Relinquishing the good for the better

There are some Christians who believe that God only ever asks us to let go of things that are wrong or may ultimately be bad for us. They believe that because God is good and wills the good, therefore, to forgo the good can never be asked of us. God only asks us to renounce our sins, never the good.

This is a surprisingly short-sighted view of Christianity for it eliminates the idea of sacrifice. This view sees God as benefactor and us as recipients with nothing being asked of us other than the joyful acceptance of all that God wants to give us.

But God not only gives. God also asks that we give in return. This giving on our part is not to equalize the relationship. It is not the balancing of the books.

The genius of Christianity is that God forgives the sinner, welcomes the wayward, embraces the stranger, heals the broken, inspires the doubting, softens the rebellious and renews those who are discouraged. God's action towards us is one of amazing generosity. We receive what we don't deserve.

If God is the God of surprises, then our giving is not playing the old accountancy game. If God's good gifts are the fruit of grace, then our response cannot be based on reciprocity, let alone on law.

Merton makes the observation that 'we may be asked to renounce even the pleasure we take in doing good things in order to make sure that we do them for something more than pleasure'.[44] He is talking about renunciation as a way of purifying our motivation so that we do things for God's pleasure rather than our own benefit.

But renunciation may involve more than giving what God asks. While giving what God asks is the act of obedience, giving what is not asked is the act of thankfulness. And renunciation may be propelled by the one or the other.

While God welcomes our obedience, he also delights in our loving spontaneity. To forgo, to let go, to relinquish because we want to please God with a joyous abandonment, is possibly the greatest gift of freedom we can ever receive. And those who practise the art of renunciation are free indeed!

Starting over again
Failure, restoration and courage

It would be wonderful if our personal development was one of steady growth. The picture of a mountaineer readily springs to mind with the easy crossing of foothills to climb steadily to reach the distant mountain top. But neither personal development nor growth in spiritual maturity necessarily follow such a neat pattern, at least that is not my experience. It also doesn't seem to be the experience of people I have met or have read about.

Growth is often not a steady progression. It is often a cycle. There are good beginnings, but somewhere we get lost along the way and have to find our way back home again.

Merton thinks this is a fundamental given. He writes, 'the life of the church in history as well as the life of the individual Christian is a constantly repeated act of starting over again'.[45]

I know what Merton is talking about.

One experience still vividly imprinted on my mind had not so much to do with failure, but with burnout. Several years of intense work with street young people and drug abusers, and with no proper rest, led to a physical collapse. With this breakdown came a spiritual darkness. For all practical purposes God might as well not have existed. And prayer was an impossibility. The heavens were unyielding like the burning sun over the Nullabor Desert of Australia. When I finally came out of that darkness, I felt I was starting the Christian journey all over again.

But in an important sense, this is not really the case. And whether we have had to start again because of sin and disobedience or because the ministries and institutions we have created have become old and irrelevant, we never quite start at the very beginning again. We will always have the wisdom of experience and failure that we did not have at the journey's genesis.

What do I mean by this? The spiritual journey is not unlike a human love affair. It is not without its optimism and naivety. When difficulty and failure come and God gives the grace not to despair but to repent and move forward, then we continue the journey all the wiser because of the difficulties.

All of this can be said much more strongly. The difficulties and failures are intrinsic to the forward journey.

This does not mean that we look for failure. That will surely come. But we look to God to carry us over the abyss so that we may continue the journey of faith with renewed hope and confidence.

Meditation

The art of attentiveness

There are many ways in which knowledge can come to us. The main ways are through being taught and by doing research. It is also possible that knowledge can come through an intuitive insight. Unfortunately, this is more rare, particularly since we live in a culture which is still wedded to a more rational approach to life.

Sadly, knowledge often remains at the informational or utilitarian level. Thus knowledge is something we possess and use. And frequently this is for instrumental purposes. Knowledge is thus a power that advantages us and which we can use to shape our world.

But it is also possible that knowledge is something that possesses us rather than the other way round. When this occurs it may be best to speak of wisdom and understanding. Here knowledge becomes personal, a part of us, even intrinsic to who we are.

When this occurs, it is appropriate to speak of the meditational process. By this, I don't mean something esoteric and something that only lies in the province of the mystics. I mean, instead, a reflective process and an attentiveness that internalizes things that are important to us.

For the Christian, meditation is either a slow and reflective reading of Scripture, particularly a key phrase or word that arrests our attention, or it is a more inward process. Merton refers to the latter when he speaks of meditation as '*awakening* our interior self and attuning ourselves inwardly to the Holy Spirit'.[46]

It should be fairly obvious that both dimensions of meditation can only occur within a particular framework or context and within a particular mindset. Our hurried lifestyle does not aid us in meditation. Nor is being still sufficient, for when we outwardly stop we often remain inwardly driven. Thus stillness must move to solitude and solitude provides the setting for meditation and a reflection that is born out of a new attentiveness.

However, I think it is important to realize that meditation does not simply belong to the sacred spaces of our lives. While meditation should focus on Scripture and also should include the movements of God's Spirit within our lives, more of life may come in view. More specifically, this includes God's providential activity in the world and the world of nature.

While reflection on the world of nature, particularly its beauty and splendour, can lead us to worship the Creator, thinking about humanity's destructive impact on the environment can lead us to a more responsible stewardship. At the same time, we are also called to reflect on the movement of history and the processes of continuity and transformation. Put differently, we are challenged to reflect on our world and its achievements and its pain.

The whole of life thus comes into the purview of meditation. We want to discern the times in which we live. We wish to understand what God's mysterious activity is achieving in our world. We would like to identify what is good and what is idolatrous so we can celebrate the one and resist the latter. Thus meditation is not simply the activity of the prayer closet, but the reflection on life in the light of God's reign.

All of Scripture
Hearing and doing the will of God

I was brought up in a home where Scripture was read during the evening mealtime. We traversed the whole Bible, including all the boring bits. As a young boy I was sometimes fascinated, usually by the 'horror' stories, but most often I was disinterested. It simply made no sense, not even the Gospels. And I was not even able to think too kindly of Jesus. Had my parents known what used to rumble around in my head during Bible reading they would have been both disgusted and disappointed.

All that changed in my late teens when Jesus became a living reality for me. And Bible reading became a joy. Lunch hours in the city were usually taken up with reading more of the Bible.

Nearly a lifetime later, nothing much has changed. I avidly read Scripture, although I am willing to admit that there have been periods where I found it as dry as dust.

Merton tells how the Trappist monks approach scripture: 'the liturgical cycle took the monk through all scripture, all the Old and New Testaments, with commentaries and explanations by greatest of the Fathers, all of it chanted and prayed and absorbed and literally *lived*'.[47]

How challenging for contemporary Christians, the majority of whom have never read the Bible in its entirety, much less have meditated on and absorbed its wisdom and have made that the motivational centre of their lifestyle!

Yet how else will we know how God wants us to live if we don't hear the Bible's challenging prophetic voice, the transformative insights of the Gospels, the heartcry of the Psalms, the lessons from Israel's and the early Church's history and the Christocentric wisdom of the Pauline letters?

I have always read the Bible in big chunks, often a whole book at a time. I am not too interested in the bits and pieces. I am more a big-picture person. But this does not mean that I don't spend time reflecting on a particular thought, idea or verse.

The burning question for me in all of this has always been: What is God saying regarding what I am to believe, how I am to think, how I should live and how to act in our world in order to make a difference?

I believe that God's word is transformative and produces a counter-consciousness. God's word does not repeat the tired old clichés of our time. It has a different melody. And produces a different song in our hearts that nostalgically reverberates with what we once knew but have so hopelessly lost.

Suffering
The journey of aloneness

No matter who we are or how charmed our existence may be, suffering will be a part of the rhythm of life.

Some people understand this better than others. Those living in poverty in the Third World are not only more attuned to this reality than the have-nots in the First World, but they are also more accepting, even though they struggle to move beyond poverty.

Others, and surprisingly some Christians, seek to deny this stark reality. Suffering according to them is not for the virtuous. They are somehow innoculated. Suffering is only for those who do wrong. This twisted triumphalistic faith has failed to understand the story of Job and the reality of the cross of Christ.

I both know something about suffering and know absolutely nothing. It depends on who I compare myself to. There are certainly those who have sacrificed more and have suffered more intensely. But finally that is not the point. Comparisons with others won't get us very far. We have to walk our own journey and seek to understand our own suffering.

Thomas Merton brings us close to a core observation. He writes 'when a man suffers, he is most alone'.[48]

This is so because when one is suffering it is very difficult to be attentive to others and it is also difficult for others to be attentive to us because they may not know how to identify with the sufferer. And the latter is so because each person's suffering bears its own unique stamp.

The extent of one's aloneness in suffering is intimately connected to the nature of one's suffering.

I caught hepatitis while working in a drug rehabilitation programme. Others also had this illness. And between us we had a riot, even though everything ached, including our teeth, and we lacked energy. This was no suffering. We had bizarre fun!!

What brought me much closer to a sense of aloneness was dengue fever with its accompanying depression. With no treatment, acute fatigue, a heightening sense of powerlessness and the frequent scurries into the emotional abyss, a sense of aloneness worked its way into the core of my being in the same way that winter coldness seeps its way into a downstairs cellar.

But all of this pales into insignificance compared to the suffering caused not so much by leaving family and friends, but by being betrayed by those whom we trusted. I had several experiences of this in Christian ministry. And because it was so sudden, so intense and so unexpected I felt totally devastated and was in emotional pain that caused me to cry out and left me doubting myself, others and God.

Of course, at the time I had no idea that any grace or benefit could flow from such experiences. I was happily wrong.

Abandonment and aloneness are equivalent to the experience of the desert – the empty, desolate and foreboding place. The place where all the normal supports are stripped away and we face ourselves in raw nakedness. Providing in that situation we are able to move beyond the expected self-pity, anger and thoughts of retaliation, we have the opportunity to come to a new place in our

innermost being. A place not only of forgiveness, but where we learn
to trust the God we feel has abandoned us.

Thus the place of abandonment becomes the place for a new
sense of connectedness with the God of the lonely places.

Desert experiences
Learning to depend on God in new ways

I have been in an actual desert. However, unlike the Desert Fathers
I did not go there to live, to pray, to fight demonic forces, to protest
a lukewarm Christianity and to look for God's future kingdom to
break more fully into human affairs. I simply went to visit.

I have always been critical of the Desert Fathers. I regarded them
as escapists from the challenges and pain of the real world. I have
always believed in a world-formative Christianity, not a world-
denying form of religiosity.

But over time I have come to regard these early Christians
differently. I have come to see, that even though I was seeking to live
with and for Christ in the midst of large urban centres, I needed to
experience withdrawal as an essential part of engagement.

Let me explain what I mean.

We cannot only be on about externalization. We also need inner
renewal and empowerment. Activism is important, but so is prayer
and reflection. And no matter how much there is to do and how
pressing the needs, we cannot continue to give if the inner well has
run dry.

Merton believes that 'the desert is...the logical dwelling place
for the man who seeks to be...dependent upon no one but God'.[49]

Here Merton is using the desert as a metaphor. The 'desert' can
be the monastery. It can also be the place of prayer in a busy family
or the practice of solitude in the office of a large corporation.

The 'desert' is not only the place for prayer and solitude that we
create in the midst of our busy and often frenetic lives, it is also an
attitude of the heart. What I mean by the latter comes by way of

analogy regarding the realities of a real desert. A desert is a place of loneliness, lack, emptiness. It is the place where our normal skills and resources are inadequate. And therefore the desert strips us bare. It may well cause death, as has frequently happened in outback Australia.

Similarly, we can experience the 'desert' when we come to a lonely place where no-one can follow, or when tragedy, difficulty or voluntary relinquishment strips us bare of our own self-sufficiency, plans, hopes and dreams.

It is ironic that this place, seemingly so difficult and bare, can become the place where we trust God more fully, experience his renewing grace and are empowered to do exploits which we would never have thought possible while we were so full of our own ideas and programmes.

Great faith

Persevering in the face of loss

It has become obvious over the years that there are people who have much too high an opinion of me. They think that because I have worked for many years with troubled young people and drug addicts and have ministered in several cross-cultural situations that I must be a person of unusual commitment and dedication.

I beg to differ. And I have good reasons for believing that these people are wrong.

The whole of my life has been characterized by God giving good things to me and adding untold blessings. A wonderful wife, children I love and respect, many great friends, interesting work, the opportunity to study, the chance to make several major career changes, the joy of working with many talented and dedicated Christians in several types of ministry, the joy of discovering and developing some talents that I never thought I had, and . . . and . . .

This of course is not to suggest that there have not been difficulties along the way. But life has been wonderfully good to me. And this I attribute to God's beneficence.

Many things have been given. Very little has been taken away. And that is why I believe that I am at best a very average Christian.

Merton tells us that 'true faith must be able to go on even when everything else is taken away from us'.[50]

I have never been tested like that. And I am not asking to be tested in that way either. I am not sure how I would cope.

Clearly Jesus had everything taken away: his ministry and his life. Yet even though utterly abandoned by his Father, he fully committed himself into God's hands at awful Golgotha. Now, that is great faith!

I know of others who have been stripped of health and dignity, who have lost loved ones and who have been vilified and misunderstood. And I know of others who have never had anything and in spite of struggle and hard work will never have anything much because they live in situations of injustice.

These people have not only maintained their faith, they have grown in their commitment.

True faith is a tested faith. True faith knows trials and difficulties. True faith continues even in the face of great odds.

Settling for less

Searching for a deeper friendship

I live the Christian life with great joy. That joy has mostly to do with the experience of undeserved grace, unsought-for blessings, the faithful commitment of friends, unexpected opportunities to bring help, hope and healing to others, and the surprises that the God of this universe brings to my life.

But I also live the Christian life with a great deal of sadness. I wish that I was more committed to the strange cause of Christ whose values and ways of doing things are so very different from mine. Like forgiving enemies, giving away your treasures, empowering the poor and turning the other cheek.

I also wish that I could respond better to the needs of our wounded world. So fractured. So unjust. Too arrogant. Still so enamoured with its technologies. And yet a world in which we are so relationally inept. A world where the ideal of the common good has fallen victim to a rapacious individualism. A world where the little ones cry for shelter and care. And where so many have wandered not only from the heart of God, but also from their own flesh and blood and from commitments made in the joy of first love.

But there is a deeper sadness. At times hard to bring to words, it meanders like an underground stream in the depths of my being. To name it is embarrassing. To leave it unnamed is cowardly. Simply put, it is a lack of trust to give my life fully into the hands of God. This demonstrates a lack of courage to walk God's mysterious way, even if it means suffering, ambiguity or downward mobility.

And so, like others, I opt for self-determination, control and making choices that have other things in view more than the saddened heart of God. I find it hard to allow myself to be led on God's narrow way since I want to know the outcomes beforehand.

And so, I settle for less.

Thomas Merton reminds us that 'many contemplatives never become great saints, never enter into close friendship with God, never find a deep participation in his immense joys, because they cling to miserable little consolations'.[51]

So why do we do this? Why do we short-change ourselves. Why opt for less than what could be?

I think there are more reasons than simply that we are cowardly. We also fail to understand God's curious ways. We understand the God of power, but not the God of weakness. We understand the God of revelation, but not the God of silence. And so we follow the God that we predictably know, rather than the God who chooses to lead us on the mysterious path that is the journey of faith. As a consequence, we become candidates for the less because we follow the God of our own making, rather than the God who gently leads us into a knowledge of his will.

But having less is not having nothing. And gaining more is not grasping for more. It is allowing God to open our hearts and hands to receive whatever he may give and learning to trust his beneficence and care.

The path of prayer
Sometimes faltering, sometimes the quickened step

I have always found the spiritual discipline of prayer to be one of my greatest challenges. This is because it has been such an up-and-down, ambivalent, perplexing and at other times exhilarating, powerful and transformative experience.

I have also found it to be just plain hard work with seemingly little benefit or fruit.

There have also been times when I have stopped saying prayers. Here I resonate with Merton's observations, 'we have to learn patience in the weary and arid path that takes us through dry places in prayer'.[52] This is not to say that I always had the patience, nor did I realize it was a path. More often than not, during these times, I felt hopelessly lost.

But in a seemingly strange contradiction, I can say that I have never stopped praying even when there were times when I had stopped saying prayers. For when I have faltered and my lips have fallen silent, there was still a cry of the heart.

This cry from the depths of my being always had to do with God. Mostly that cry was: Lord, I am so discouraged; I am so tired and confused; I am so overwhelmed; I am so lost and I cannot find you. And on a more positive note: Lord, I do trust in you even though you seem so far away; please hold me and help me; see me through this present darkness; and bring me again into the light and joy of your presence.

Happily, the path of prayer is not always so agonizingly difficult.

In prayer I have also felt sheltered and nurtured. I have received wisdom, insight, guidance and direction. And in times of intercessory prayer I have later learned that God actually intervened in situations.

But whether the path of prayer is easy or difficult it is an essential part of the Christian life. Prayer as an act of faith joins us to God. It links us to God as worshipper, penitent and seeker, but also as participator and friend.

Prayer is the appropriate language of the creature to the Creator. It is also the language of friendship and intimacy.

The hidden life

The pursuit of spiritual intimacy

Thomas Merton describes Trappist monks as 'men who lived hidden in the secret of God's face'.[53] He is referring to their life of prayer and contemplation.

But is such a life possible for people who are living ordinary lives in society? Is it possible for them, despite their duties and responsibilities of family, neighbourliness, work and citizenship, to live in God's presence? Potentially, the answer is, 'yes'. Practically, the answer is, with great difficulty.

The degree of difficulty has a lot to do with the busyness of daily life. Family, work, church and community responsibilities fill our lives, making incessant demands so that we find ourselves rushing from one thing to the next, but never being able to give adequate attention to all the things that come our way.

But we are not only busy. We are also distracted. This is not to suggest that the two ideas are not related. But one can be busy and not distracted. One can be busy and prayerful, peaceful and focused at the same time.

While being distracted may well have something to do with our outer world, it has much more to do with our inner world. It occurs when our compulsions remain unguarded. Our frustrations unresolved. The hunger for more unabated. The conflicts irreconcilable. The hurts unforgiven. Our pain unhealed.

The need to settle our inner conflicts is often far more pressing than resolving our supposed lack of time.

And if we can, by the grace of God, still the raging 'demons' within, a life of intimacy with God becomes a vibrant and exciting possibility, even in the midst of demanding routines.

We can be at prayer while at work. We can be with God in the midst of a seminar or a board meeting. We can be in communion with the God of all grace while talking to other people.

And times for solitude and prayer can be carved out of our busy routines so that we can seek God's face in a more focused and concentrated way.

If we regard intimacy with God as intrinsic to our very existence and the dynamic of our life, then sheltering in God's presence can become a normal part of our lives.

BEING WITH
The Search for Friendship
and Community

In the first section of this book, we spoke of the search for self-identity. In those pages we celebrated our being made in God's image, our uniqueness and the blessing of personhood. In the following section, we acknowledged our search for transcendence and our need for the transformative activity of God in our lives. In this third section, we explore the blessing and challenge of friendship and community.

At the heart of the biblical story lies a Trinitarian faith, the vision of a God who builds a people, of Christ who formed a community of disciples and of the Spirit who breaks down the barriers and makes us one. Scripture speaks of the Church as a community of equals and everywhere in the Bible's pages we hear of the importance of relationships with God, family, brothers and sisters in the faith, the neighbour and with the stranger who is in need.

Being human necessitates the acknowledgement of the importance of relationships. Through others and in companionship with others our life is formed, shaped and enriched. And while the relationships on the horizontal level – family, friends, colleagues, neighbours – are of great importance, so is the vertical relationship where through the grace in Christ we form a friendship with Father, Son and Holy Spirit.

While the gift of family is basic and enduring, the blessings of friends are important in our becoming what we are meant to be. Friends who are there for us, who wound and challenge us in love, who succour us and support us through the vicissitudes of life are a gift beyond measure.

Similarly, the gift of the community of faith is formative in our growth in maturity and in conformity to Christ. In a life together of word, sacrament, worship, nurture and care and service, our life of faith is sustained and empowered. Moreover, in this companionship we can grow in our understanding and experience of the reign of God and encourage each other in living the strange upside-down values of the kingdom of God. In this kind of solidarity we can serve the world as a sign and sacrament of the grace of God.

Relationality lies at the heart of Merton's thinking. The Trinity is a sign of the fraternity of the human community and the work of the Spirit forms and sustains the faith community.

Merton gave much of his life to companionship in a Trappist monastery, and his vast correspondence gives evidence of the many friends to whom he gave and who in turn blessed Merton's life.

The matters of relationality and community are particularly pertinent for our present context. Many of our relationships have become denuded and reduced to functionality. We are respected for what we do, not known for who we are. Much of our urban landscape has become dysfunctional and our social fabric is deeply torn.

While we might wish that the Church be different, this is hardly the case. Shaped by an easy believism, structured after the corporate world and functioning to serve consumer interests, the Church is hardly an example of a life together that reflects the Trinity and the example of Jesus.

Many Christians hold at best a loose relationship with the Church and have superficial relationships with each other. Many are ecclesiastical orphans.

The challenge of community calls us to a deep conversion. Moving beyond the self-preoccupation that so characterizes our contemporary age, Christians are challenged to a life together that involves mutual care and sharing. This means sharing prayers and resources. It involves mutual confession and encouragement. It includes a commitment to stability and being willing to walk the long journey with our brothers and sisters in Christ.

The world desperately needs to see a Christianity of embodiment, of words made flesh in a solidarity through the Spirit. Such a community is a sign and sacrament of the kingdom of God and a place of shared leadership, gender equality and empowerment of the laity and is a community that seeks to wash the feet of the world.

A dangerous memory
Community in early Christianity

Thomas Merton informs us that 'Cistercian monasticism is a communal ideal which goes back explicitly to the life of the first Christians who were of "one heart and one mind" and "had all things in common".'[54]

Of course, it is not only the Roman Catholic religious communities that have been inspired by the Jerusalem experiment recorded in the book of Acts. The Anabaptists, the Moravians and many expressions of Christian community since the 1960s have all found their impetus in the story of Acts 2 and 4.

In fact, throughout the long journey of the Church there have been continual attempts to give concrete expression to the community ideal. And while there have been problems and excesses, the Church has often been most relevant and has made its biggest impact when it was structured as a caring community.

For many, however, the concept of Church as community is regarded as a rather quaint but outmoded ideal. It is seen as a hangover from the mediaeval world with its agrarian simplicity. And therefore it is seen as the province of monks or of religious fringe groups who find delight in pointing the finger at mainline churches.

But community need not be relegated to the realm of the bizarre. It can be seen as a mainstream reality.

Community can be built in families, friendships, support groups, churches, educational institutions and the workplace. Community can be built anywhere where people are together and in relationship.

While most of my experience has been in living in therapeutic communities, I have also experienced community in the marketplace. And the one has been as enriching as the other.

Community has to do with a sharing of place, relationships and interests. Community begins when we develop relationships of openness and trust. It grows when reciprocity develops and we move into the gentle cycle of giving and receiving. Beyond that, community may express itself in differing models of shared lifestyle and mission.

God is a community. And Christ in word and sacrament

expresses himself in community where people from different social and economic backgrounds find a common life together of prayer, teaching, fellowship and service.

Building community
Creating a better world

Building community is one of our greatest challenges, for community is the mosaic of human sociality. Simply put, we are communal creatures and therefore we build friendships, families, networks and all sorts of associations.

In building these frames of relationships we express an ancient and archetypal memory long forgotten by the majority in our secularized Western culture. This memory deeply embedded in the Christian tradition speaks of the fact that we are all creatures made in the image of a Trinitarian God who is a community of persons. So whether we are building a general neighbourliness so necessary in our urban lifestyle of fragmentation and alienation, or whether we are specifically building a Christian faith community, both spring from this ancient memory.

This of course is not to suggest that all forms of community are the same. The community of family is not the same as the community of friendship. Neighbourliness is not the same as belonging to a Christian community. But there are some similarities in this web of relationships.

The most fundamental elements in building any form of community are presence and shared communication and openness. Community has to do with being *with* others. But it is a particular form of being with. We can be with others and yet remain detached, uninvolved and disconnected. This may be true of workplaces, neighbourhoods and also of Christian churches.

Mere presence is never enough.

We need to learn to be present to others and this involves openness and sharing.

Thomas Merton, who lived the monastic form of community, is adamant: 'mere living in the midst of other men does not guarantee that we live in communion with them or even in communication with them'.[55] In other words, the very structure of an intentional form of Christian community does not of itself guarantee that community in the fuller sense will occur.

While we need to be clear that there are no guarantees for community, since community is finally a gift of grace, the key challenge in building community lies in the phrase – to be present to others. And clearly, this is something that in the final analysis cannot be organizationally and institutionally regulated.

To be present to another person can only flow out of the magic of love. One loves and therefore communicates, listens, joins, shares. One loves and is therefore willing to make common journey with others. One loves and is willing to enter the places of pain and need.

And one is loved. Community is multi-directional. It is sharing a common life. It is sharing common bread. It is life together.

This does not mean that all are equally strong nor that all have much to give. Rather, it means that we may give and receive depending on where we are in the journey of life. Those who are strong will not always be so. And those who are weak may well be towers of strength in times of difficulty.

Face to face

Community and maturity

At first glance there does not seem to be an obvious connection between community and maturity. Living with others may well create dependency and irresponsibility when community is an escape from the world and when certain strong people dominate.

My experience of community has been quite different. While I in no way wish to idealize community, community has been the place for encouragement, growth and service.

Thomas Merton makes the observation, 'it is by well-ordered

contact, by relatedness with others, that we ourselves become
mature and responsible persons'.[56] He, of course, is writing out of
his experience as a Trappist monk. I write out of the experience of
living in various therapeutic communities which provided a safe
place for young people coming out of drug addiction and
prostitution. Yet our observations are similar. Community provided
a place of growth not only for those with life-controlling problems,
but also for us who had the joy of joining with them in their journey
towards wholeness.

Living with others provides us with self-insight, for in the face of
the other we more fully recognize ourselves. Moreover, the
uniqueness of another person's journey and struggle can open some
of the closed areas of our own life.

But when community is structured for friendship and care, a
sharing of our natural talents and spiritual gifts, and facilitates a
willingness to serve and encourage each other, then community
becomes the safe place where we can grow and extend ourselves to
embrace new challenges and ways to serve the wider community.

Community is not an escape from the problems of our world.
Instead, it is a place for empowerment so that we can re-engage our
world with new-found energies and courage.

Becoming mature and responsible means not only that we make
our contribution within the community of faith. It also means that
we can embrace some of the wider concerns of our world because
we know that God's sheltering presence in the midst of brothers and
sisters fuels us with new-found faith and hope.

Solitude

Power in community building

I have lived most of my life in various forms of intentional Christian
community. This had nothing to do with a failure or scepticism
regarding family life. Family is God's wonderful gift to humanity.
Family is also a form of community. However, in our contemporary

world it has become a most fragile institution. Being families and singles in community can greatly strengthen the family.

However, such pragmatics cannot be the sole purpose for forming Christian community. Community comes out of a theological vision. God is a community of persons, and this God is at work in the world building a people. And these people of God are called to be a sign and sacrament of who God is, and they do this not simply by proclamation but by demonstrating in their life together something of God's reconciliation and healing.

While we are called to build community reflecting the Trinitarian God, community will always be a gift of grace and a miracle of the Spirit's renewing work. Moreover, even though community may express itself in particular historical forms, such as Benedictine monasticism or the pattern of the L'Arche communities, the existential experience of community will always be fragile. For while community may have a particular structure, its heart is the ability to love those with whom we share our lives. And this love needs to be received and given again and again in the face of our ever-ready selfishness and self-preoccupation.

Thus while certain structures can express a particular form of Christian community, structures in and of themselves cannot form the heart of community. This comes from prayer and contemplation. This may sound surprising for some who believe that it is service that builds community. While service, like structures, is important, service must come from a good place! It can't, if it is sustained simply from habit, duty or guilt. It must come from a deeper and better place.

Thomas Merton reflecting on his own experience as a Trappist monk, writes, 'it is in deep solitude that I find the gentleness with which I can truly love my brothers'.[57] Why is this so? Because in the daily round of being in a community where one sees faults and weaknesses, where one may fail to respect others' differentness, and where one does not see the realization of one's own ideals, it is so easy to become negative and critical.

And the solution for all of this is not toleration, but transformation. In the quiet place with a quiet heart through the stilling of the inward storms by the breath of God, one can find grace for forgiveness, for perseverance and for hope. Solitude, the birthplace of hearing the voice of God leading to the exclamation of our prayers, forms the heart for community-building – for it is there that we find the fuel for the journey of a common brotherhood and sisterhood.

The practice of forgiveness

Releasing ourselves and others from pain and anger

That I have hurt other people and will do so again is a foregone conclusion. A reoccurring pattern of pain had to do with my inability to deliver what other people expected of me. Somehow, I must give the impression that I can do more than what I am capable of doing. There are of course many other ways in which I have hurt others, including people who are very close to me.

That others have hurt me is also stating the obvious. The greatest hurt was the betrayal of trust that I had placed in leaders and workers with whom I was in ministry. Since loyalty is a big issue for me, its violation causes me great pain.

It also needs to be said that I have hurt myself, as much, if not more, than what others have done. That we sin against others and that others sin against us is one thing. That we also sin against ourselves is another.

My greatest sin against myself was the failure to deal with my compulsions and drivenness. I simply took these with me into my Christian experience and validated them under the guise of Christian service. As a result, aspects of my Christian service had more to do with my drivenness than with my dependency on the love and grace of God.

Therefore, I was good at giving. But not so good at receiving. Leading, but not at being led. Talking, but not at listening. Doing things, but not at celebrating life.

Forgiveness has everything to do with dealing with the pain we have inflicted on others, that others have inflicted on us and that we have meted out to ourselves. When we have hurt others we go in humility to seek their forgiveness and we live out the fruit of our repentance towards them. When others have hurt us we forgive them irrespective of whether they come to apologize or not. And when we have hurt ourselves we need to learn to become gentle with ourselves and change our ways.

Forgiveness is the staple food of our existence. It is the grace we don't deserve. It is the magic that makes the ugly beautiful. It is the dynamite that unlocks the deadlock. It is God dancing into our tired world spreading goodwill and reconciliation.

Merton reminds us that 'the most difficult and the most necessary of renunciation [is] to give up resentment'.[58] And forgiveness is the magic key that does precisely that. So let us forgive as we have been forgiven by the God of all grace and mercy.

The whole Christ
Christ existing as community

I am not particularly good at connecting up with people. I am more of a loner. My family upbringing undoubtedly had something to do with this. We were not very close and individualism was strongly encouraged.

What I learned about warmth in relationships came from my wife's family and the home life she created for our own family.

It was this experience of family that led to participation in various forms of Christian community. And while community had its own particular pains and struggles, the benefits and joys of life together far outweighed the difficulties.

Good community is the safe place where we can be nurtured, encouraged and challenged. Such a place not only gives us a deep sense of belonging, but draws into the discovery of gifts and qualities that we didn't know we possessed.

But community is much more than this. It is the place where we learn not only about ourselves, but also about God.

Merton tells us that 'each of us will find God in his own way, but all of us together will find him by living together in the Spirit, in perfect charity, as members of one another in Christ'.[59]

In Christian community we may discover the whole Christ. As we worship together, share the insights of Scripture together, share common meals together and participate in the Eucharist, pray for one another and share each others' burdens, share common resources and find ways to serve our broken world, we discover so much more of the Christ among us than if we pursue our individualistic ways.

Christ exists as word, sacrament and community, was Dietrich Bonhoeffer's claim. And in sharing life together, we can experience so much more of the Christ who came not to be served, but to serve and give his life as a ransom for many.

Withholding

Maintaining the gentle art of privacy

Having had the privilege of living in Asia for a number of years has made me realize with greater clarity how verbal we Westerners are. We want to make everything explicit. We talk everything out, virtually to the point that the personal becomes public exposure. And we see many examples of the lives of the rich and famous becoming fodder for a gutter press which celebrates the banalities, idiosyncrasies and indiscretions of their lives.

By way of contrast, Asians seem to be more implicit in their communication and leave a lot unsaid or more subtly implied. This is a refreshing contrast to the verbosity of many Westerners, myself included.

But even though I enjoy expressing myself as a preacher, teacher or writer, I am also a strongly private person, and only my family and some close friends really know me well.

And I like being private. I enjoy living in my own inner world. I enjoy being by myself. I feel happy with the thought that there are things that belong to me and not to everyone else.

Merton puts it very simply, 'there are things one doesn't talk about'.[60] While he may well have had specific things in mind when he made this statement, I wish to draw out some practical implications.

While it is true that life is all about sharing, it is also about withholding. So what should I withhold? That of course depends on the kind of relationships I have with others. With those with whom I have a very close friendship I may share most things. With one's spouse one would probably share everything.

But we also have our inner thought-world. We also have hopes and dreams. These may need to be safeguarded. Some ideas may take a long time to mature. Others need to be thrown away. To talk frenetically about anything and everything may be a way of undermining our inner world. Nothing ever gets a chance to become consolidated.

Since honesty and openness should always be coupled with discretion, we will always need discernment to know what to share and what to withhold.

The friend
The gift of a companion for the journey

The more that we sense the greying and flattening contours of the way dominant culture shapes our soulscape, the more we want to celebrate and highlight our uniqueness and individuality. The latter, pushed to an extreme, can make a fetish of our idiosyncrasies and push us into unhealthy isolation.

Friendships are a wonderful counterbalance to this. This is not to say that this is the sole purpose for friendship. Friendship is a value in and of itself: a friend is a wonderful gift who is celebrated and appreciated, not because she or he may help us to overcome certain unhealthy tendencies, but because he or she gives us the gift of companionship.

While we may be able to enjoy quite a number of friendships at various levels of intimacy, we may also be blessed with a special friend who is especially close. This soul friend, or whatever special designation we may wish to use, becomes as important to us as life itself.

Thomas Merton in his journals writes of one such person. 'Dom Porion seems to be the one person in the world that I have actually come to have as a friend who has an interior life that rings bells inside of me.'[61] This appears to be a special friendship of similarity where closeness is predicated on identical personality or similarity of interests.

I also know of such friendship, but the more significant for me has been the friendship of difference. In one sense, such a friendship could hardly be because of the many differences. As a result, such a friendship was the surprise. The magic gift that comes unexpectedly.

The value of this kind of friendship is that the other always appears as 'other' and therefore brings freshness and the unexpected to the relationship. While sameness can bring the blessing of stability and continuity – great gifts indeed – differentness can bring the blessing of challenge and transformation. Moreover, the sense of mystery predominates in this latter kind of friendship, while boredom may become the bane of the former type of friendship.

A friendship of difference, however, does require hard work. It requires good listening. It requires a willingness to hear a different perspective and often invites us into ambiguity. It necessitates an inner security. People who are insecure are seldom able to hear the other. But there is a richness in this kind of friendship because it pushes us beyond familiar horizons.

While the differences may be those of gender, culture or vocation, the differences of personality and life perspective may be the most fruitful. While there may be vocational similarities, the exchange of differing life perspectives makes life rich.

Thankfulness

The joy of affirming what others have done

I am sure we all have met both. The person who is very self-confident and very self-sufficient and the person who is very dependent.

It does not necessarily follow that the one is very arrogant and the other extremely thankful. One can be self-confident and thankful and one can be very dependent and sullen and angry.

To put that differently, it is possible to have much and to be very thankful and to have little and to be unthankful. It simply does not follow that those who have little are grateful and those who have much are ungrateful, although both are possible.

Thankfulness, ultimately, has nothing to do with whether one has much or little. It has to do with an approach to life that is celebrative rather than sullen or resentful.

Thankfulness springs from a recognition that we deserve nothing, but that we have been given much. This is not to say that we have all been equally blessed, for that is simply not the case. And to start comparing ourselves with others is a sure way to remain unthankful.

Life remains fundamentally unfair despite God's providential care. A poor couple may be blessed with many children, while a more well-to-do couple may be barren. While there is a strange irony in this, the one family can find joy in their children and the other in different blessings that God has given them.

Since life is God's gift, and family is the good gift of our parents, and resources are the blessings of God's good earth, and friendship is the good and gentle gift of others, then there is already much that we can be grateful for.

This is not to say that we may not or should not reach out for more. But if gaining the more robs us of our sense of thankfulness and joy, then we have regressed rather than progressed.

Merton gently reminds us that 'my first human act is the recognition of how much I owe everybody else'.[62] It also remains my last act. And this recognition causes me to celebrate how much I have been given and how good God is.

Seeking Christ in the face of the other
Learning to truly see

Being a Christian has nothing to do with becoming a bigoted religious fanatic, even though some right-wing fundamentalists give that impression. At the same time, being a Christian does not mean being an anaemic chameleon who fits in with whatever way the cultural wind blows.

Being a Christian means to be deeply connected to God while at the same time being fully human and participating in all the joys and challenges that life brings relationally and socially.

To be immersed in God finally does not draw us away from engaging in all of life. In fact, with God we can take life in full stride.

The Christian in engaging the neighbour and the work colleague should not bring an air of superiority or a spirit of judgementalism. Instead, we are challenged to bring understanding, compassion and a deep desire to know the other person and to be a blessing.

The reason for this open and generous attitude towards others is because the Christian lives in the light of God's grace, acceptance and generosity.

To know God is not some tiresome religious routine. While church may sometimes be like that, God is never like that!! God is the One who enters our lives, surprises us with forgiveness and grace, empowers us with his Spirit and sends us dancing into the world.

With God we may enter the world with wonder and look all around us for the signs of his creativity, goodness and care. We can stoop to admire the one-day bush lily. Ponder the starry heavens. Rock a sleeping baby. Admire a piece of art. Fondle one's lover. Be pensive with a reflective piece of music. Have raucous laughter with friends. Be amazed at the skill of an athlete and admire the creativity of a colleague.

Having come home to the heart of God by faith, we turn our gaze again and again to discover the heart of God not only in the place of meditation and prayer, but also in the rhythms, joys and ordinariness of our daily lives and of our world.

Thus we go into the world to find. We are the gazers not into a crystal ball looking for the magical answers of the future, but as those who look for the signs of God's love and light even when so much of our world seems dark.

Thomas Merton makes the observation that 'every man is, to the Christian, in some sense a brother'.[63]

He is right. We should see every person as made in the image of

God and therefore as persons of dignity and equality, irrespective of race, gender, education, training and temperament.

Every person is the potential beneficiary of Christ's redemptive and reconciling work. And therefore every person bears the hidden mark of Christ. In everyone we may see the hidden Christ.

But this sadly does not mean that every person has accepted God's kindness and embraced the life that Christ gives.

But our aching longing for others is that they may acknowledge the light that is already shining upon them. Eat at the table set out so bountifully. Receive the gift so gently and freely offered. Drink at the fountain flowing with the elixir of life. Welcome the renewing power of God's Spirit.

And so we go into the world with eyes full of wonder and hearts full of longing. Everywhere we see the signs of hope and in every young or haggard face we see the contours of the hidden Christ about to burst forth into fullness of life.

The mentor
Being guided by the wisdom of others

Psychological tests typify me as the most independent of all the personality types. There are both blessings and disadvantages in this fact. One obvious advantage is the ability to be self-motivated and to get on with the task even when others are not interested or supportive. An obvious weakness has been my failure to listen to the good advice of others.

I have slowly learned the importance of listening to the input of others and seeking advice, counsel and help. I only wish that I had learned this earlier in life.

This is not to say that I have always formally had a mentor. Although I don't believe that I stand under Merton's judgement that 'the most dangerous man in the world is the contemplative who is guided by nobody'.[64] It is not that I disagree with the intention of his statement. It is just that there are many ways of being guided by others without necessarily entering upon a formal mentoring or spiritual direction relationship.

I have found much wisdom and help in the marriage partnership, the blessing of long-term friendships, life in Christian community and journeying with particular Christian authors.

For a long time, Rita and I have made no major decisions without seeking the input and prayers of friends and the significant others in our lives. And I have the joy of relationships where I can fully be myself, open my heart, share my pain and seek advice regarding major future plans.

The fruit of operating in this way is so obvious and worthwhile that I can't understand how earlier in life I could have been so stupid as to think that I did not need this.

One of the great blessings in life is to be in solidarity with others. This involves not only close friendships, but also mutual accountability. There is nothing more wonderful than a community which cares and nurtures, but also facilitates growth. And there is nothing greater than friendships which are accepting, but also challenging.

In these contexts one can be secure, and because of this stability, one can embrace great adventures and challenges. Having truly come home one can go forth knowing that others not only have contributed to the decision, but will continue to be there for you in hard and good times.

Overflow
The art of generous service

Something very strange happens in the spiritual life: we look for blessings for ourselves, yet we are asked to give them away. This seeming paradox invites us to embrace the heart of the gospel where giving becomes receiving and death issues into life.

Thomas Merton reminds us that 'any joy that does not overflow from our souls and helps other men to rejoice in God, does not come to us from God'.[65]

This does not mean that we cannot and should not give to God alone. Prayer, worship, adoration are, in one sense, for God alone. God is most worthy to be praised for who he is and all that he has done. But surprisingly, the worship of God also blesses and empowers us. In worship, we are not simply drawn out of ourselves and out of our world with all its concerns, but we are also drawn into God's presence. Presence means connectedness, and this brings peace and life.

There is also a sense in which we should seek things for ourselves. We need God's forgiveness and grace. We need encouragement in difficult situations and in the long journey that we all must walk. A journey which so often is marked by stops and starts and frequently by sidetracks and unexpected hindrances. We also need nourishment and empowerment and healing from life's hurts and pains.

Thus we need much. And one of the first movements in the spiritual journey is to acknowledge our need of the God of all grace.

And life's secret is to continue to admit our needs. Nothing cuts us off more deeply from the sources of the spiritual life than the false idea that we are somehow complete and in need of nothing. Such a person is clearly caught in the gloom of a lack of self-knowledge and in the nightmare of a misunderstanding of the grace of God.

But to have our needs met can never remain simply with ourselves. Being forgiven we forgive others. Being blessed, we bless others. Being healed, we seek to be the instruments of healing to a broken world.

When life is given, it can also overflow to others. Blessings, then, translate into acts of service. And in the giving away, more will be given to us.

Thus the greater our knowledge of God, the more we are called to teach others. The more we have received in material well-being from God's beneficent hand, the greater the challenge to empower the poor.

The gospel while it first of all calls us to God also calls us to move outside of ourselves to the care of others.

No matter how much our contemporary culture maligns altruism, the gospel always calls us to hospitality, generosity and service.

Overflow is, therefore, not a demand. It is a simple consequence of the abundant life that God gives us. Freely we have received; freely we may give.

Failure

Facing our imperfections

I have spent more of my life living in various forms of Christian community than I have being part of the traditional Church. This is not because I am disillusioned with the traditional Church. I just happen to believe that Christian community is a better structure in which to nurture and disciple marginalized people.

Christian community is always tinged with a certain amount of idealism or utopian thinking. Many contemporary Christian communities see themselves as an expression of the communities of faith of early Christianity. Others see themselves as a prophetic sign to the Church and the world calling for a more participatory lifestyle. Others see themselves as expressing a greater level of care and concern for brothers and sisters in Christ than what normally occurs in the institutional Church.

I am happy to admit that I have also come to Christian community with an unreflective idealism. Inspired by the long history of monasticism, the painful history of Anabaptism and the inspirational example of the Moravians, I believed that community could better serve the vision of the kingdom of God.

While my own experience of Christian community has been overwhelmingly positive and growthful, it has not been without pain and failure. The greatest failure for me has been the failure of friendship.

Thomas Merton soberly reminds us that 'as long as we are on earth, the love that unites us will bring us suffering by our very contact with one another, because this love is the resetting of a Body of broken bones'.[66]

Christian community is not only a sharing of care, gifts and resources centred in a common commitment to Christ. It is also a sharing of our life journey, idiosyncrasies, pain and incompleteness.

We can assume too much. Take too much for granted. Expect too much. As a result, we meet at the level of our expectations and not at the level of the way things really are. And so we may well hurt each other rather than being the instruments of healing and encouragement.

At best, Christian community consists of broken people journeying together in their quest for wholeness and in their desire to serve the world.

Holism

Experiencing and celebrating all of life

As I am learning to become more reflective, I am becoming more aware of the amazing connectedness of life. This connectedness has not only to do with the relationships between my mind, emotions and body, but also my connectedness with others and my environment.

When I am with certain people I come away energized. With others I simply feel drained. Certain settings – particularly nature untouched by human hand – speak a language that is understood in the very depths of my being, and this is the language of encouragement, nurture and empowerment.

Merton warns us not to reduce the richness and complexity of life to singular factors or answers. He writes, 'there is no place for the cultivation of . . . *one aspect* of human experience at the expense of others'.[67]

Sadly, this happens so often, particularly in the Western world with its perverted love for priorities. Rather than seeing spirit as important as reason, and family as occupation, and reflection as work, the latter categories are so often emphasized to the sad neglect of the others.

But the secularists in suppressing the spiritual dimensions of life are not the only ones to blame. There are plenty of people who embrace a spirituality who show a blatant disregard for the more normal realities of life. While secularists may reject the art of spiritual healing, the religious may give scant attention to exercise, proper diet and concern for environmental pollution.

God's good gifts include the gift of life, family, friends, community, the Church and society. These good gifts are sustained by the created order and shaped by human care and stewardship. All of these gifts are interrelated. Therefore each of these gifts should not only be appreciated, but guarded as well.

We cannot only build up the Church without also being deeply involved in the realities of society. Just as much as we cannot only be concerned about our soul while we neglect the body.

The quest for holism is the gentle but difficult art of integration. Complementarity rather than competition is its genius. And it constantly seeks the blessing of the whole rather than the elevation of the part.

Aloneness
Allowing for the empty spaces in our lives

My memories of childhood are not filled with people, although I had plenty in my life including friends, grandparents, aunts and uncles. Growing up in the old former university town of Franeker in Northern Friesland was to belong to a close-knit community. But my dominant memories were of an inner world, not a world of people and events, and my most precious times were being alone in the nearby fields which hung as a colourful woman's skirt around the old town centre.

This sense of aloneness has never left me, in spite of the fact that I have experienced the closeness of my own family, the solidarity of Christian community and the joy and challenge of working together with many wonderful people in various ministry situations. To these I have felt deeply connected, and yet I have always felt apart.

Merton came 'home' when he entered the Abbey of Gethsemani in Kentucky, USA. Yet he writes, 'this is my place and yet I have never felt so strongly that I have "no place"'.[68]

This sense of feeling apart or having no place has nothing to do with aloofness or an arrogant distanciation. This does not spring from an inability to form healthy interpersonal relationships. Nor does it originate from an implicit sense of superiority. While these things may be the case in unhealthy motivations, in more healthy personalities aloneness is the productive place.

Unfortunately, most of us will do anything we can to fill the empty places and to crowd our lives in order to block out this sense of aloneness. While at face level this is most understandable, it robs us of some of our potentially most enriching experiences.

Let me explain.

Being alone literally means to be in a place devoid of other people – an empty place. This can also occur in the midst of people through a process of inner distanciation. Since we are people who long for social solidarity, aloneness creates in us a hunger for intimacy and this can drive us to an intimacy with God that we will otherwise never know if we constantly fill our lives with people and a myriad of activities.

But aloneness is also productive in other ways. Since aloneness involves outer or inner distanciation, it means that we can step back from the dominant values of our age, the tyranny of the urgent, the demands of the present and the pressure of the immediate. In creating this kind of space we have the opportunity to rethink, evaluate, dream some different dreams and possibly come to see things in a new light.

Thus aloneness is not only productive for our relationship with God, but also for making a more prophetic stance in this unjust world of ours.

Openness and hiddenness
The quest for true friendship

I am quite sure that we have experienced both.

The intrusive person. Known or stranger, it matters not. But wanting something from us. The what of the wanting often unclear to both of us. Pressing. Probing. Desiring what we do not want to give. Or wanting what we may not even possess. We feel their questions like icy probes around our hearts. And their unarticulated demands bind us rather than free us to love and participation.

We feel vaguely violated and disempowered. And we come away from such encounters uneasy and confused. Sometimes guilty. Wondering whether in fact we have failed the other person.

We also know the other person. Non-demanding. Freeing. We are comfortable and at peace with each other. There are no driving hidden expectations. There is only the happiness in being together. There is room. There is respect. There is the sacredness of distance and joining.

Merton comments, 'if I love a person, I will love that which most makes him a person: the secrecy, the hiddenness, the solitude of his own individual being, which God alone can penetrate and understand'.[69]

Friendship and intimacy can never develop and grow under a probing and pressing demand for the nakedness of the soul of the other. The opposite is in fact the case. Intimacy can only become fruitful in the context of freedom and respect of the sacredness of the other person.

True friendship involves a gentle unveiling. It cannot be a rushed intrusion.

But none of this implies that we simply wait our time for the scraps of self-revelation like vultures who wait for their share of the pickings. We don't wait for more. We accept what has been given in friendship and love. We honour the level of revealedness with a sacred trust. But we equally honour the levels of hiddenness which are the sanctuary of the other person's being.

Friendship does not strip the other, because true friendship can't be based on an all-knowingness. It can only be based on a love that trusts. And a love that trusts is a love that guards.

While some things are appropriate for the confessor or for one's spiritual guide, not everything is appropriate for a friendship. Constant openness becomes more the bleeding wound than the seedbed for healthy growth.

But when the sacredness of the other is truly guarded and openness operates on the basis of freedom and not demand, then surely two people will grow in the undress of the soul.

Guidance

Listening with discernment

No matter how deeply we are embedded in our family, neighbour-hood or community of faith, there is something fundamentally lonely about being a Christian. At least this has been my experience.

This is not to say that God is not with us nor that we lack brothers and sisters in the journey of discipleship. It is recognizing something quite different, namely, that each of us must finally walk the road of obedience. And while that road is often in solidarity with others, it may also be a lonely road.

Somewhere along the line, I have to decide what it is that God is calling me to do and I have to have the courage of my convictions to begin to live that out.

This does not mean that I come to these important decisions by myself. I do need the input and encouragement of others.

Merton warns us about turning to certain people for help. He writes, 'no one will entrust himself to the guidance of men who have never had to suffer anything and have never really faced the problems of life'.[70] Put positively, we can and should turn to those who have walked the road ahead of us. And while not unscathed, they have continued in faith and hope even while wounded and at times overwhelmed.

I have a number of such friends.

What is always so delightful in talking and praying things through with these companions is that they never come with ready advice and easy answers. Instead, they come much more with questions and with reflections on the pain and struggle of their own journeys of faith.

The other thing that is so fantastic about these friends is that they are prepared to back me no matter what decision I finally make.

This has not always been my experience with others. In fact, I have found some Christians to be very manipulative. They have given advice that fits their interests and have given support that benefits their particular church or ministry.

Thus in the difficult process of getting direction for our lives we need to be open not only to the leading of God's Spirit, but also to the input of others. In listening to these various voices we need discernment and we can only have that when we stand in a place of freedom and not of constraint.

Being alone
Coming in touch with our inner core

By temperament, I am an introvert, even though by vocation I am very much a public person. And though my life has been filled with people, particularly through living in various forms of Christian community, my inner life has also been nourished by the experiences of aloneness. My childhood memories are filled with being alone in the fields of Northern Holland and my young adult memories are full of the grandeur of the mountains of Southern Queensland. It was not only that I lived in these places. I chose to be there by myself. I needed to be there alone.

One can also be alone in the city, or even in a crowd. And one can find quiet places in the midst of a very busy life in order to be with oneself and with the God who shelters and nurtures us.

Merton reminds us of the need to find 'a place where your mind can be idle, and forget its concerns, descend into silence, and worship the Father in secret'.[71] In one small sentence, he is saying a lot, for being alone is not for sullen isolation and withdrawal, but for unwinding and unburdening in order to be refreshed through worship and adoration.

For me, being alone has to do with restoring my inner equilibrium which becomes unsettled in the process of externalization in the busy round of teaching, tutoring, mentoring and counselling. It is vital for me to be with myself in the quiet place.

But being alone means a lot more than this. Finding one's centre is one thing. Finding new energy and creativity is another. In the quiet place, I am able to hear things to which otherwise I am deaf. I can feel things which normally I suppress. And new things emerge which normally would have been aborted.

The reason why there are so many blessings in the quiet place has something to do with learning the art of solitude. But it has more to do with drawing near to God. Being alone is not being abandoned. It is coming home. It is being with the One who made us, loves us and who is committed to our well-being and spiritual growth.

A place

Finding the safe places of transformation

Place is very important to me. It comes out of the recognition not only that I have a body in which I need to be at home, but that I am part of places and spaces where I incarnate my existence. These places provide a rootedness to my life and they shape me just as I may also impact the places I inhabit.

A place, where we create family and community, where we share life with neighbours, or where we work or play, is God's good gift to us. A gift that provides the framework in which we can express who we are in the light of God's beneficence. A context, in which we nurture and develop human relationships. And a resource that we may use to practise hospitality and thereby bless others.

I think that places are especially important to me because I have moved so much: from Europe to Australia, from there to Asia and then to Canada. And because I have lived in rented houses, I have moved many more times than those who continue on in the family home.

A place, whether that be a house, an office, a garden, a special spot in a municipal park, needs to have a certain beauty in order for me to feel at home. I am not talking about a grandiose or expensive beauty, but one that in its simplicity reminds me of the gift of light and life that God has given.

Thomas Merton not only found his sense of place in a Trappist monastery, but found his special place within its sacred walls as well. He writes: 'My chief joy is to escape to the attic of the garden house and the little broken window that looks out over the fields.'[72]

I have also found or created the special smaller places, whether that was a particular spot near a river or a corner of a room.

These smaller places are important to me because it is there that I spend time to be still, to reflect, to meditate and to pray. In that sense, these become the sacred places which in another sense look ever so ordinary.

The very entering of those particular places already moves me towards the purpose of why I am there. Thus place becomes a medium and support for one's spiritual disciplines.

As a young man working in the printing and publishing industry and having just come to faith in Christ, I can still see myself day by day coming to work early and sitting in my favourite corner where I could see the rest of the office and the crowded streets below. There I came to read Scripture and to pray and to think about how all these other people at work and in the street below might also make the great discovery of new life in God.

Little did I know that some time later Bible studies at work would bring others to faith and that I would spend many years walking those very streets involved in urban mission.

God inhabits the special places, which need not be our church sanctuaries. These can be any place in the midst of our busy lives where we create space for solitude and prayer.

Spiritual direction
The value of another's voice

In many ways our contemporary society encourages us to be alone, because we are to be self-sufficient and independent. Moreover, competition rather than cooperation is so much a part of the way we live and act. This is true even in our educational and religious institutions.

In living this way, our relationships with others, including our teachers and our pastors, are always at a distance. We are happy to receive the other's expertise. We may even be willing to accept advice. But being open to receiving guidance is a whole other matter.

Not only are we reluctant at this point, but our relationships don't facilitate open and vulnerable interaction. We relate to others in terms of our strengths, competencies and achievements.

But this is a one-sided and dangerous way to live. We also need relationships where we can be vulnerable and receive direction. It is here that the role of a spiritual director can be so significant, helpful and empowering.

So while I recognize the value of friends who give feedback, support and encouragement and the role of the clergy person who can provide pastoral care, and the skills that a professional counsellor or psychologist can use on our behalf, the ministry of the spiritual director is to be valued and welcomed.

Over the years, I have had the benefit of both having a spiritual director and being able to serve others in this way, particularly students. It's a great blessing that someone is willing to listen to my story and my life issues and throw some light on those areas where I am particularly blind. Just as it is a great privilege for me to journey with others as they wrestle with identity, directional and spiritual issues.

Thomas Merton believes that the task of the spiritual director is to be concerned with the whole person, and therefore he/she is more interested 'in the basic attitudes of the soul, our inmost aspirations, our way of meeting difficulties, our mode of responding to good and evil'.[73] The task is not particular problem-solving, but discerning the movement of the Spirit of God in a person's life and what is life-giving as opposed to death-dealing.

Spiritual direction is fundamentally a careful and prayerful listening to what the directee may wish to share. This listening may result in asking questions that open up wider perspectives. It may also result in a respectful acceptance. But the direction of the entire interactive process is towards a fuller discernment regarding the wholeness to which the directee is drawn and the growth to fuller conformity in Christ.

No director or spiritual guide is in any way sufficient for such an awesome task. Hence the need for humility and dependence on the Holy Spirit – the Spirit of discernment. Spiritual direction occurs in an environment of respect and trust. It is also a setting of grace and not of judgement. But above all it is the place where the light of God's wisdom penetrates all the dark places, bringing hope, release and direction.

A strange redemption
Being blessed in the blessing of others

Depending on the various and curious cycles of history, humanism moves from virile optimism to a tired and sagging despair. Times of war with all its dehumanizing atrocities move us into the spiral of the latter. Times of peace, prosperity and progress tend to generate a greater optimism.

While I believe in the dignity, worth and creativity of the human being, I am not impressed with the humanistic project. Not only is it too vulnerable to the movements of history, but its underlying assumptions are untenable. That we are somehow basically good, and the sum of all things, is both naive and arrogant. What is closer to home is that while greatness lies at our fingertips, chaos and the dysfunctional are in our hands.

As a result, I believe that we are prime candidates for redemption and transformation. And while we have innate capacities for growth and self-improvement, redemption must come outside of us in order to renew us. This is the heart of the gospel. God the persistent and pursuing lover reaches out to welcome wandering sons and daughters home, drawing us by the Spirit and using the pain and difficulties of life to move us from our self-sufficiencies to an openness and vulnerability.

In Christ, mediated by the Spirit, God's redemptive love comes home to us and draws us to our true home, to live and be in God's presence. But this renewal cannot be or become a static possession. It is to be an ongoing dynamic in our lives.

This dynamic needs to partake of the strange action of God. God works through weakness, self-giving and a shameful cross. The King serves. The living God in Christ dies. And the power of resurrection is the surprise of faith. Similarly, our ongoing redemption, renewal and transformation, while the gift of God, comes with the cost of self-giving.

Thomas Merton notes that 'when we extend our hand to the enemy who is sinking in the abyss, God reaches out for both of us'.[74] In other words, our ongoing renewal is bound up not only with God, but also with our brothers and sisters in Christ, and the stranger whose shadow we barely acknowledge.

In forgiving, we are forgiven. In blessing others, we are blessed. In serving the community of faith, we are renewed in our life together. And in serving the poor, we are serving the poor, hidden Christ in them.

Western individualistic Christianity has lost the sense of the corporate nature of God's redemptive activity. For them, it is simply a matter of what God has done for me. But God calls us to be a people, builds us into a community and welcomes us to be dependent on his grace and interdependent on each other. Moreover, God works through others his wonders to perform.

The Pilgrim Church
Christian community in a desolate world

Christians in the First World are now by far the minority of Christians in the world. While the Church in the Third World is not without its great struggles, including the pain of poverty, it has a virility and authenticity which is lacking in the First World.

This does not mean that the Church in the First World is facing its final demise. But it does mean that it is in grave difficulty, needing transformation and renewal. What that renewal should look like is the subject of a cacophony of voices. But some reoccurring themes can now be heard.

The first and most basic is that the Church in the West needs to recover the uniqueness of the gospel and live out a more authentic Christianity. For too long the Church, for the sake of relevance, has attempted to be like the world in the hope that the world as a consequence would then like Christ. Thus the Church has been more like a social welfare society or a club rather than the house of God. The consequence of this is much-needed renewal in that the Church needs to be more fully converted and transformed by its own message.

A second theme is that the Church needs to recover a vision of community. Moving beyond the individualism of our contemporary society and the preoccupation with institutional models, the Church is challenged to become a community of equals; where God is worshipped; where women and men may lead; where life together is practised; where the poor are welcomed; and where the wider community is engaged in loving service. This calls for a move beyond the consumer Christianity so characteristic of the West and calls for the formation of covenant communities where our lives in Christ are formed, nurtured and empowered.

A further theme has to do with a recovery of new forms of integration and holism. Western Christianity has long been plagued by unhealthy dualisms. Soul and body. Heaven and earth. Prayer and work. Church and world. Spirituality and politics. The list is endless, but the aftermath of this kind of thinking is a faith that partakes more of Greek idealism than the earthy, incarnational spirituality of the Bible. This together with the Western propensity for categorization, departmentalization and specialization has fragmented our understanding and experience of what it means to be the body of Christ that lives in the Spirit, by the Word, in worship, nurture, fellowship and service.

A final theme picks up an emphasis of Merton. He writes, 'the monastic church is the church of the wilderness'.[75] Merton has monastic communities in view here with their isolation from mainstream society, their liturgical practices, their life of prayer, solitude and work. And of course, the monastic vision of obedience, celibacy, poverty and stability is in view as well. This perspective is important for the mainstream Church. This is not to suggest that the contemporary Church becomes monastic. But it does need to become impregnated with a monastic spirit. This means that the spirit of Christendom needs to be exorcised. This is the acceptable, popular and powerful Church. This the contemporary Church no longer is, nor can be. Instead, it is to be the Church of humility, prayer, lament, poverty. It is to be the Church of the present difficult time. The Church of the wilderness. The Church praying and watching for God's redemption.

BEING AGAINST
The Search for a Prophetic Voice

There are many people who live an inherent conservatism. They accept the world and life as it is. They believe in the goodwill of those who lead and serve us and accept the basic institutional realities that shape and sustain all of our lives.

There are others who are critical and even deeply sceptical of the dominant values of contemporary society. They question both the vision and motivation of those in political and social leadership. And they are unhappy with many of our social institutions, believing that these only favour those who already have much.

Sadly, there are also those who simply don't care. Their primary concern is with themselves and their families, but the wider political and social questions are of little interest.

While these three groupings do not exhaust all the possibilities, they do set some of the contours. What we may ask is, where do Christians fit into these categories? While Christians from the Montanists through to the contemporary liberation theologians have sought to be agents of change and transformation, often Christians have lived a dull conservatism.

It seems to me that Christians are called to fit into none of these three categories. They present the possibility of a fourth option. And this option becomes a possibility when they inhabit and live out of the biblical vision. That vision sculpts a profound respect for the created world as God's handiwork. It celebrates all that is good in the social order as the gifts of God's common grace. But it also recognizes the deep faultlines in our personal lives and in the social fabric. It faces the human tilt towards self-gratification, autonomy, the misuse of power and the capacity for self-deception and idolatry. In the face of these bitter realities, the biblical vision accents the God who joins the fray, who enters history, who redeems his people, who empowers the poor, who has a passion for justice and who seeks the healing and restoration of the whole created order.

Therefore, Christians can never be the third grouping. They cannot be those who don't care since the God whom they worship cares passionately for the redemption and restoration of all things, including individuals and families, but also the institutions and social order that sustains and shapes our lives.

Christians cannot be the first grouping, either. While they rightly celebrate and appreciate all that is good in our world, they cannot be blind to its evil and idolatry, including the evil in their own lives. Conservatism blesses what is, including our own contributions to evil and injustice. This cannot be, since the God of the Bible calls us to overcome evil with good. The biblical vision is the call to repentance and to live the reign of God. This calls us to be the agents of transformation, not the servants of conservatism.

If there is any single group to which Christians could belong, it is the second. But this requires important qualifications. Christians are not critical of their world out of mere negativity or a rebellious spirit. Nor are they critical through the embrace of an ideology that, while it offers a utopian dream, finally brings enslavement and oppression. Instead, Christians are critical of themselves and of their world in light of the hope that God's Spirit will bring renewal that issues in reconciliation, peace, justice and the embrace of the poor.

What all this means is that Christians impacted by a vision of the Kingdom will live that vision in their communities of faith, and will seek in loving service to carry the Kingdom to others and to the social realities of our time.

This calls the Christian community to the task of discernment and to the gift of prophecy. The exercise of this gift never *begins* with critiquing our world. It begins in contemplation, becoming attentive to God, to our own lives and to the pain and dysfunctionality of our world. It then issues in our own repentance and in sacrificial and committed incarnational service. Out of this, prophetic speaking may emerge.

One cannot read Thomas Merton but be struck by his surprising engagement with the world. This Trappist monk, 'hidden' in the monastery, is not someone merely contemplating heavenly things but unattentive to the issues of our time. Rather, the one dimension impacts the other. The vision of God draws him to the neighbour. The plight of the neighbour draws him to God.

Merton prayed and wrote about the need for the reform of monasticism, racial reconciliation, peacemaking in the midst of warmongering, and wrestled with many of the deformations caused by our urban world and the use of technology.

While we may not wish to follow Merton regarding the specific issues of his social concern, we are challenged to search for a prophetic voice. We are not simply called to bless, but also to discern. We are not only to affirm, but also to challenge. We are not called only to announce good news, but also to denounce the idolatries of our time.

Those who watch
Waiting, praying, discerning, speaking

There are powerful forces at work in our contemporary world that move us to conformity. Globalization spreads the message of Western cultural values and central is the idea that being compulsive consumers of the glittering trinkets of our economies will give us the happiness and sense of well-being that we are all so desperately seeking.

These forces promoting conformity are also evident in our educational and political institutions. The former shape people to become not thinkers but practitioners to serve the capitalist enterprise, while the latter have jettisoned all ideological considerations to deliver bland policies based on economic rationalism.

Sadly, the contemporary Christian Church has not been able to resist the seductive power of these values. In fact, the Church in the West has become culturally captive. As a result, its internal life has become weakened. Without theological dialogue, Scripture-based preaching and formative spiritual disciplines, the Church provides religious services that are less than engaging and transformational.

While the Church is called to be a counter-cultural community living the shalom of God's reign, and as such is called to be a prophetic witness to the wider society, it first of all needs to be converted. This is a painful journey. It is never easy for the healer to acknowledge woundedness and the need for transformation.

If the Church is willing to move to a new humility and a renewed prayerfulness, its very vulnerability may well become its new strength. The prophetic voice of the people of God does not arise from the places of power or comfortability. Instead, it emerges from the place of conversion, the place of waiting, the place of crying.

Merton in one of his poems speaks of monks as 'planted like sentinels upon the world's frontier'.[76] They are not simply the prayerful guardians of their own community. They are not simply the worshippers of the Trinitarian God. They are also there for the sake of the world. And their calling is not only one of acting in faithful service to the world, but also one of prayer on the world's behalf.

While only some Christians are called to become monastics, all are called to prayer and to the art of discernment. And these two disciplines are closely related. In prayer, we express our dependence on God and his Word and catch a glimpse of his kingdom. Discernment involves seeing all of life in the light of God's reign.

The prophetic task does not come from a life of busy service, but from contemplation. Its first task is not to speak, but to listen. Prophets are sentinels who look to God and to the world and whose message brings the light of God to the darkness of our world, including the darkness in the Church.

Contemporary Western Christians need a reawakening in the power of the Spirit who calls us to wait, pray, listen, discern. And who will empower us to act and speak concerning God's redemptive and transformative concerns for our world.

At the margins

Seeing life from a different perspective

I have always felt myself to be a bit of an outsider. There are undoubtedly many reasons for this. As a young boy, I was a migrant kid. In my early twenties, I worked among marginalized Aborigines in inland Western Australia. In the Church, I have always been regarded as a bit of a radical. And much of my ministry has been with problem people at the edge of society. These realities I have internalized.

I am neither proud nor despairing about this. This has been the direction of my life and these are some of the choices I have made. There have been particular blessings in this journey and particular pains as well.

One recurring blessing is that life at the margins helped to give me a different perspective on many of life's issues. It also helped me to join with others who are struggling. And it has somehow drawn me to God in a way that may not have been possible had I been located more centrally in positions of power.

The long saga of pain and struggle has been to remain faithful in often despairing situations and to challenge more centrally located institutions to become more responsive to people at the margins. This was frequently a hopeless task and led to misunderstanding and sometimes further alienation.

I have many not-so-fond memories of being called up before a Church committee or a government tribunal having to explain certain positions and actions I had taken.

Merton makes the relevant observation that living as a monk 'you become a completely marginal person in order to break through the inevitable artificiality of social life'.[77] A monk by the life he chooses to live says 'no' to so much in normal society, including marriage, a work career, possession of private property, and a life of freedom and consumerism.

However, there are also other ways to be part of a prophetic minority. There are many lay communities who are ministering to the needy and marginalized. And there are many individuals within the system who live their lives by the sound of a different drummer.

At the margins one may well discover insights and blessings that are also good for those located in positions of power.

A *disturbing presence*
Asking the difficult questions

Oh, yes, like you, I have met them. The narrow drum-beaters. The
fervent flag-wavers. People who champion marginal causes and
promote them with a zest as if the salvation of the whole world
depended on them.

I have also met an array of self-styled prophets. Blindly out of
synch with everyone else, but super-confident that their causes were
the only issues worth fighting for. But, I am not talking about any of
these!

When Merton states 'you must be willing...to become a
disturbing...person, one who is not wanted because he(she) upsets
the general dream',[78] he does not have bigots and ratbags in view.
Nor self-styled prophets. Nor narrow fundamentalists. Rather, he is
speaking about the reluctant listener to a different drumbeat who
dares to raise a voice when the cacophony of voices is reduced to a
faulty monologue.

Despite the collapse of some of the major metanarratives or
ideologies of our age, spurious secular gospels are still promoted
with boring repetition. Individualism, consumerism and militarism
have hardly become mute in the plurality of voices in our time. But
the need for disturbing persons, who are out of step with our
dominant values, has little to do with the entertainment of adding a
dissonant voice. Something much more serious is at play here.

We all know that fair play and justice stumbles ever so easily in
the political, social, educational and religious institutions of our
land. We also know that pristine visions easily deteriorate into a
humdrum conformity and that altruistic projects become, over time,
the domain of the self-advancers. The move from innovative
charism to deadening routinization is everywhere writ large on our
social landscape.

These situations don't necessarily require abandonment, but they
do need transformation and renewal.

Therefore we need people of insight, humility and courage who
dare to ask the difficult questions. Who are prepared to visit again
the sources for the original inspiration. Who are able to suggest

ways to move forward to adapt to changing circumstances without negating the original vision.

Such people are a great gift to any group, community or institution. But because they are a disturbing presence, their contributions are often negated by a cloud of suspicion or reaction, rather than embrace and welcome.

Thus, these prophets must be willing to walk the difficult and lonely road seeking to serve truly in the face of suspicion and rejection. In this, they take risks that insight brings and are called to carry its burden with dignity and grace.

The deepest centre
God at the core of our being

There are those rare moments in life when we can see beyond the immediate and the pressing and see things with a lucidity that puts everything in a different perspective.

There are obvious reasons why these moments are all too infrequent. Most of life we simply take for granted. We have internalized the world as we see it and experience it. And we often tend not to question the obvious and what is close at hand. Nor do we generally question the most fundamental realities of our social world. That's the way life is, we so frequently say without probing the magic possibility that life could be different.

Merton in a moment of great clarity writes, 'why should joy excite me or sorrow cast me down, achievement delight me or failure depress me, life attract me or death repel me, if I live only the life that is within me by God's gift?'[79]

This vision looks beyond all the excitement and struggles of our social self to find our integration point in who we are in the new life we have received in Christ Jesus.

Coming to this perspective involves the gentle but difficult art of relinquishment. It means that one has been able to move below the surface of life's normal preoccupations to touch an inner core of truth and certainty, even though this certainty is premised on faith.

This magic discovery has nothing to do with our own insight and wisdom. It is a sheer grace gift of God. It is the piercing moment of truth that rips away the masquerade of so much that we normally hold as important.

Discovering that the centre of life does not lie in the normal gamut of our many activities, but in being close to the heart of God, frees us to be new persons with a very different vision of life and with very different agendas.

This provides the 'revolutionary' impulse of true Christianity. Not an impulse to bring about change through violence. But an impulse to change through following the One who has given us life and in whom we have lost our lives.

The greatest change agents are not the social activists, but the contemplatives who have been transformed by a vision of God and who seek to live out that vision in our tired and broken world.

Non-conformity

Re-listening to God's radical story

I have often been regarded as a bit of a 'radical' and 'rebel' by people within the community of faith. I find these designations rather amusing. If people only realized how conservative I am at heart, they would never have used these sorts of labels. Not only have I been shaped by a conservative family and social ethic, the formative brand of Reformed theology that shaped my early understanding of Christianity was hardly known for its radicality.

But of course, more shapes us than simply our beginnings. As we develop, we also begin to see the world with our own eyes. And while some continue to embrace the world with a largely unquestioning acceptance, others begin to see the world more critically. I belong to this latter group.

The reasons for seeing life more through the grid of a

hermeneutics of suspicion rather than a hermeneutics of consent are twofold.

First, the reading of the gospel impressed upon me the stark reality that both the religious and political institutions of Jesus' day failed to see the manifestation of God's greatest good in the gift of his Son and instead colluded to eradicate him. While I do not wish to suggest that all institutions since are equally non-discerning and evil, I do believe that God's kind of good calls the values of the world into question. God's kingdom of righteousness, forgiveness and peace is very different from a world where exploitation, control and self-interest are the marks of the secular gospel. Thus, we need to be critical of the kind of world we are shaping.

Second, anyone who has worked with the poor and marginalized in either the First or the Two-Thirds World, realizes that the poor as a whole are the victims of exploitation and the self-interest of those who have power. Seen from the perspective of the poor, there is nothing fair or just about our world. And with the gap between rich and poor ever widening, there is no indication that shalom will come to those who have the least.

This widening gap, God's good news calls into question. For everywhere in Scripture is writ large the astounding perspective that God's concern is for the poor, the weak and the needy. The little ones are the focus of God's history while the great ones are the focus of our history.

God's story focuses on the Hebrew slaves in Egyptian captivity, the disempowered ones in the history of the Israelite kings, and on the marginalized in the mission of Jesus. While God's good news is for all, it is the poor who draw near to the Kingdom, and the rich resist because they refuse to become the little ones for the sake of the Kingdom.

Merton makes the observation that 'to conform is not to act well, but only to "look good"'.[80]

This can be put much stronger. To conform is the failure to choose God's narrow way.

What makes conformity unacceptable is that we fit in to what the dominant ethos of our culture demands, when instead we are called to resonate with God's heartbeat for our world.

Non-conformity to the values of our age is only possible to the degree that we do conform to the way that Jesus lived and live the lifestyle of his kingdom.

Traditions
Renewing our heritage

While Roman Catholics are comfortable with the idea of tradition, Evangelicals tend to get nervous. The latter often have the strange notion that they have no traditions because they claim to go back beyond tradition to the ethos of early Christianity. While this may be a laudable ideal, it is first of all going back to a tradition that forms the beliefs, ethos and ethics of early Christianity. In other words, early Christianity is itself a tradition, or more accurately a set of traditions because the ethos of the Matthean communities is not the same for example as that of the Johannine communities.

But second, Evangelical Christianity is not only shaped by its interpretation of the New Testament, it is also shaped by the way Evangelicalism came into being, by its history, and by aspects of the modern world.

Moreover, the picture is even more complex. Evangelical Christianity itself contains a variety of traditions even though there may be a common core. Fundamentalist Evangelical Christianity looks quite different from prophetic Evangelical groups seeking to wed evangelism and social concern and justice issues. And there are also differences between First World Evangelicals and those from the Two-Thirds World.

But tradition shapes not only major denominations, but also local churches. The ethos and feel of a local church is as much shaped by tradition as it is by gospel.

Tradition is a fact of family, institutional, cultural and social life.

The issue, therefore, is not doing away with tradition, as if we can. Rather, the issue is discerning whether our traditions continue to serve us well.

They don't, always!

Merton's observation is therefore relevant: 'human traditions all tend towards stagnation and decay. They try to perpetuate things that cannot be perpetuated. They cling to objects and values which time destroys without mercy.'[81]

The long history of Christianity has demonstrated both the power of tradition in its continuity right up to the present, and the need for tradition's renewability.

When traditions are no longer life-giving; no longer empower people; no longer reflect the strange values of God's upside-down kingdom; and when they are no longer relevant as an embodiment of contemporary understandings of faith and life in the light of the gospel, then traditions need to be renewed from within.

Here Roman Catholics have tended to do a better job than Protestants. The former have been more inclusive and have been able to incorporate change and renewal. Protestants have tended to be more exclusive and intolerant of change and renewal occurring within their traditions. As a result, splinterization has continued to be a feature.

Instead of seeing change and renewal as a threat, we need to see it as the breath of God bringing new life to jaded structures and practices. Communities of faith should truly be ever-renewing entities. Renewed by the gospel and the Spirit of God and by the thirst for relevance, the Church can truly seek to be a signpost of the Kingdom of God.

Where renewal is resisted, the increasing intolerable old will bring decay. Where renewal is embraced, the pain of new birth will bring new life.

Disconnections

Developing a critical awareness

One of the key ideas within the Christian community has to do with right relationships. We are to be rightly related to God, to ourselves and to others if we want to live in a wholesome and integrated way.

This key idea is undoubtedly valid since relationality lies at the heart of who God is – a God who is Trinity and who calls people to worship and obey him. It is also central to the concept of Christian community – brothers and sisters joined through Christ to form a common place of worship and witness. But this concept is also important for the social order where cohesion is necessary lest society splinters into myriads of shards causing social fragmentation. There are limits to pluriformity!

But connectedness is not the only important idea. Disconnectedness is also a critical component of well-being, growth and spirituality.

Not only is the meta-story of the Bible replete with the formation of a people, but it also knows of the solitary ones – particularly the prophets – who are to be set apart. To be disconnected.

The purpose of disconnection has nothing to do with an attempt to undermine or to destroy peoplehood or community. In fact, the motivation is precisely the opposite. It has to do with the renewal of community through disconnectedness. Merton writes that the person 'who wants to deepen his existential awareness has to make a break with ordinary existence, and this break is costly'.[82]

Put differently, critical self-awareness which is essential to growth and development, necessitates an ability to disconnect and to create distance. If one is always absorbed by what is happening in one's immediate environment and is always responding to needs and issues then these things become the determining realities of one's life. Disconnectedness and critical distance are not to be avoided, but should be purposefully cultivated. They are not the bane, but are a part of the blessing of the spiritual life.

The biblical meta-story knows not only of the city, but also of the desert. It knows the story of a people, but also of the prophet who cries out his passion for God in the wilderness – Prepare ye the way of the Lord! This disconnectedness is not meant to feed a sullen aloneness, or an arrogant sense of differentness. Quite the opposite! The purpose of withdrawal is to become sufficiently uncluttered in order to gain an awareness of different voices. The voice of the ideal, rather than the social self. The voice of hope so frequently suppressed by the voices of fear. The voice of passion so often sidelined by the voice of convention. The voice of the good so seldom heard above the voice of the convenient.

And soaring like an eagle above all of these voices is the gentle and penetrating voice of God insisting on a way of being and doing that has an eternal kingdom in view and a present lifestyle that forgives, serves and empowers.

Thus, blessed are the disconnected ones who flee to the heart of God! And believing the whispers of another world, find the courage to call this world into question and to build the world to come!

The other prophet
Listening to the voice that is against us

We are usually enamoured with the familiar, even though that may invite regular bouts of boredom. The familiar not only gives us a sense of comfortability, but it also buttresses us against our deepest fears and insecurities. And so we inhabit the familiarities of place, culture and relationships.

While we may wish to explore beyond these familiar places, we are usually quick to return to them again. Or what is more frequently the case, we take the familiar with us, and even though we are in unfamiliar places, the familiar still predominates. Westerners often live as Westerners overseas and consequently learn nothing from the host culture.

What also frequently occurs is that we merely sample what is foreign and different and quickly assimilate it to our own values. As a result, we learn little and nothing much changes. The dominant paradigms of our own making remain intact.

In religious circles, the voice of the familiar and the voice of tradition frequently predominate. The sanctuary is the place of peace, rest and security. We come to church for reconfirmation, not for transformation. With all the changes going on around us, particularly in the workplace and in the global economy, we don't want the place of faith to also be the place of change.

And yet, change we must. A lively faith is a renewed faith. It is

also a relevant faith. And therefore, faith needs its own transformations and one way in which this can occur is through the challenging
voice of the other.

The other may be a renewed reading of Scripture which comes to
us with new power and relevance. The other may also be the
dramatic coming of the Spirit, turning our familiar world upside-
down and filling us with new zeal, vision and power. The other may
also be the secular prophet who reminds the Church to live with
integrity.

In whatever way this other voice may come to us, it is a voice for
us that is against us. It's the voice that comes from a new place and
shakes the comfortability of all our familiar places. This voice brings
rupture, but not to destroy, rather to heal.

There is nothing easy about hearing the voice that is against us.
Its very disturbance brings fright and unease. Our willingness to
listen calls for great humility and openness. In one sense, this voice
is the voice of death for it calls us into an unknown and not
previously traversed path.

The problem with creating and listening to our own prophets is
that they only speak in familiar tones. They don't call us to renewal
and transformation. It is the other prophet who comes to disturb.
Merton reminds us that 'God is to be heard, not only on Sinai, not
only in our own heart, but in the *voice of the stranger.*'[83]

Sharing the world's anguish
Bending our ear to God and the world

I have often wanted to turn away and turn a blind eye to the need
and brokenness of those around me. Many years of working with
drug addicts and street people, and then the long haul of seeking to
bring healing to those suffering from various forms of trauma and
abuse, have often left me overwhelmed and depowered.

The thought has often been there: This is enough. Let others do
it. Live a different sort of lifestyle.

Now I am not talking about the legitimate need to withdraw for a while in order to find renewal and strength for the ongoing journey. I am talking about giving up. But for me, at least, this was impossible, for this kind of lifestyle is somehow linked to my understanding of what it means to follow Jesus, who came to bring healing, deliverance and empowerment for the poor and the little ones in our world.

And so the journey has continued with the ever-present challenge to find sources of renewal in the midst of daily life and ministry. If we can't always take our tired self to some ideal and idyllic spot for refreshment and renewal, then we need to bring ways of empowerment into the rhythm of daily life.

Here, we can learn from the monks. While they appear to have left the needs of the world to others, the vocation of the monk is not to forget the world. Rather, in their calling to be at prayer, while removed from normal daily life, they can better intercede on behalf of the world.

Thomas Merton points out that 'the monk in spite of his essential solitude, can be open to the needs and to the anguish of the world'. Such a person can take upon himself or herself 'the sins and conflicts of the world' through a 'Christlike unselfishness and purity of heart'.[84] The application of this to all those who are social activists is that they need to be contemplatives just as all contemplatives need to have a heart for the world.

The practice of solitude, prayer and reflection is not simply to give us new energies for the many and seemingly unending tasks that constantly beckon and sometimes threaten us. In the act of contemplation we are also drawn to worship. And how much we need to learn the upward glance when we are so preoccupied with the issues and needs of our time!

But the contemplative gift also has critical relevance. To disengage and to bend our hearts once again to the God of all grace and wisdom and to hear whispers from the world beyond and to be empowered with new dreams and possibilities, is a way of seeing our world anew. And how much we need this when the daily humdrum of need can paralyse us to the point where we cease to ask the hard questions.

The work of transformation needs to be done in hope, and hope cannot be a naive optimism but must be a vision of the doable in the light of faith.

Marching to a different drummer
The journey of relevance without comformity

As a Christian I have always felt pulled in opposite directions. On the one hand, I am mesmerized by the strange upside-down values of the kingdom of God. On the other, I am attracted by the sheer functionality and practicality of the best our modern world has to offer.

This tension runs through many other aspects of my life. I enjoy contemplation. But I love action as well. I enjoy being with God, but with my human companions as well. I love reading theology, but I equally love philosophy and literature. I have enjoyed working in the Church, but also in various secular occupations.

Fortunately, I don't have to resolve these tensions since loving God does not put me in opposition to my neighbour, and working in the secular marketplace does not mean that I am no longer God's servant, particularly not since I desire to be salt and light wherever I may find myself.

Being a Christian does not preclude immersion in the world. But it does involve resisting the worldliness of the world.

Since Christianity is essentially a world-formative religion, rather than a world-denying one, the challenge is not safe withdrawal, but relevance without conformity.

Thomas Merton reminds us that 'the basis of the Christian mission to the world is precisely that the Christian is "not of this world". He is first freed from its particular myths, idolatries and confusions by his Christian faith.'[85]

This unshackling is a process. The worldliness of the world has seeped deep into our very being. We don't immediately recognize the idols of our age. Nor do we readily unmask the false ideologies of our time. And we certainly don't easily come into contact with our own social sins of bigotry and racism.

But that this unshackling and de-masking work has to occur, is without a doubt. We don't add much to the well-being of the world if we simply baptize its idols.

Since the Christian task is essentially transformative, we need to have a different vision of the way the world should be. This vision should embody kingdom values and display mercy and justice.

The challenge for us, therefore, is to become more godly, less worldly and more loving and focused in our attempts to respond to the needs of our world.

Renunciation

Learning the gentle art of letting go

I have always felt that living the Christian life involves me in a strange paradox. On the one hand, I am called to be responsible and proactive. This follows from the creation mandate where God calls me, and all other people, to be vice-regents under his lordship. This involves seeing the continuity of family, the well-being of society and care for God's world.

On the other hand, I am also called to be prayerful, trusting in God, and not to be self-reliant. And while I am to be very much involved in playing my part in this world, I am not to become enamoured with the things of this world. In fact, I am called to resist the powers of this age.

Living with paradox, however, also occurs at a more deeply personal level. This has to do with the strange interplay between holding onto certain things and thereby losing them and relinquishing things and becoming the recipient of unexpected surprises.

Some, and particularly those with a 'bless-me' form of spirituality, have sought to reduce this mystery to the level of technique. They preach the doubtful dictum that when we give certain things to God, similar things will be given back to us. This form of bargaining reduces our relationship with God to a crass commercialism.

Merton, however, invokes the mystery of faith when he writes, 'by renouncing the world we conquer the world'.[86] Or to put that a little more accurately, in renouncing the world, we do not allow the world to possess or control us.

While I don't claim to understand this paradox, I have entered into it.

I have had the experience of letting go a good and well-paid position, sensing God's call to work overseas in a voluntary capacity and to find unexpected and amazing blessings. It's as if the relinquishment of the one freed me to receive God's surprises.

Renunciation and relinquishment is a form of detachment that breaks the power of the immediate, the pressing and the dominating realities of our lives, which frees us for a re-engagement. This re-engagement is always new and different because our empty hands have been filled with God's new things.

Dealing with contradiction
Questioning, struggling, trusting, surrendering

It is virtually a dictum to say that the person who has not experienced life's contradictions is a person who has not lived. And we don't have to go looking for the unexplainables of life, they come knocking on our door. More frequently, they simply crash into the living room of our lives.

While there are any number of intellectual contradictions, such as how can we reconcile God's sovereignty and goodness with the appalling lack of justice in our wounded world, it is the existential contradiction that affects us the most for it impacts on us in our daily living.

I have the proverbial filing cabinet full of such contradictions. Does that not mean that these things are neatly filed away? No, they are part of the ebb and flow of my life. While some contradictions are more occasional, a more persistent one has to do with the observation that when things seem to be going so well in ministry or in the community of faith then things are already on the downhill slide. It seems that at the peak of our success the rot has already set in. Thus the very things that we are working so hard to achieve are the very things that are our undoing.

Thomas Merton observes that 'we are not meant to resolve all contradictions, but to live with them and rise above them'.[87] This does not mean passive resignation. On the other hand, we cannot always fight the unwinnable.

While we are meant to make sense of our world, we will always have to face mystery, complexity and contradiction. But contradiction need not be the mother of despair. It can be the handmaid of humility. We need not deny the contradictions of life in order to bolster our fragility and insecurity. We can face life boldly with our questions and struggles.

The contradictions of life may lead us to a careful prayerfulness that dynamites our pride and confidence in the systems and institutions we create and in the drunken power of success. As such, contradiction defines our vulnerability before God and can be God's tool in overcoming our propensity to human idolatry.

To pray is to acknowledge mystery. To face the contradictions of life is to become a candidate to seek the wisdom of God.

God's will

Anxious load or light burden?

I have often looked with wonderment and a certain amount of incomprehensibility at people who happily breeze through life. I have also doubted their openness and honesty, for they always claim that everything is fine.

The reason for the latter evaluation is that this is not my experience of life and therefore I have doubted its possibility for others.

All of this, of course, is a huge mistake on my part. Why should others experience life the way I do? And just because I tend to travel in heavy weather does not mean that others cannot enjoy the light breeze!

This more heavy and sombre approach to life may well have something to do with my beginnings in the dour Friesian landscape of Northern Holland and my rather serious Calvinist upbringing. Calvinist Christianity is hardly known for its frivolity and joy!

My coming to faith in Christ brought new freedoms and blessings, but did not fundamentally change the way I operated in the world. As a result, doing the will of God has always been a heavy journey for me, rather than lighthearted and joyful steps in following the Master.

I say this with a certain amount of sadness because I don't believe that what I have made of the journey of faith is necessarily how God means it to be.

I often feel that I have walked through mud and slush when I could have taken the high road or even had eagle's wings.

Merton writes that 'we easily persuade ourselves that... what is easy is my own will: what is hard is God's will'.[88]

As I have indicated, I have tended to function along these lines. But a fault-line runs through this approach. Doing my will is ultimately never easy. It is just plain foolish. Living without God's direction is living without God's benediction.

At the same time, it does not follow that God's will is simply difficult. It is the wisest thing to do and the safest place to be.

The God who has made us and renews us in Christ is the God who not only calls us on the journey of faithfulness, but also sustains us along the way.

Conformity

Resisting its subtle power

Thomas Merton in expressing his concern about conformity writes, 'the noble Christian concept of duty and sacrifice must not be debased to the point where the Christian becomes the passive and servile instrument of inhuman government'.[89] This concern should also be extended in various other directions. It is not only government which can be inhuman. Sometimes institutions can be oppressive. This can also be true of the Church when it is governed more by ideology rather than by the gospel.

Historically, Christians have been more oriented towards social conformity and promoting social stability than to social critique and social transformation. The reasons for this need to be carefully understood, particularly now that we are living in a period of history where society has become so fragmented that change is urgently called for.

The question we need to pose is as follows: How is it possible that Christians are so frequently sociopolitically conservative when the founder of Christianity, Jesus Christ, sought to radically renew Judaism, initiated a new movement, proclaimed the radical ethic of the Sermon on the Mount, brought in the kingdom of God's reconciling love, formed community and empowered the marginalized and poor?

There are a number of ways of responding to this most basic question. The first is the general observation that over time renewal movements with their vision of new beginnings become rationalized and institutionalized. This is also true of Christianity. The radical egalitarian vision of the Jesus movement and of the Pauline house churches becomes dulled with time, and we end up with a diluted vision and diluted forms and structures.

The second response is that our faith, the reading of Scripture and the understanding of the Christian life are shaped by the churches we are a part of. The Church thus mediates the gospel to us, filtering it through its contemporary structures and experience. To the extent that the Church is not fully teaching and living the gospel, to that extent we, the Church's members, will be robbed of the radical power of the gospel.

A further response is that the Church makes much of the notion of obedience. In the case of Jesus this was a radical obedience to the Father's will in bringing in the Kingdom and going the painful road of the cross. In our case, obedience is one of affirming and reinforcing held values, beliefs and practices. In other words, an obedient person is one who fits in with a given authority structure. Thus the Church rewards conformists and bureaucrats and rejects the radicals and the revolutionaries.

Our duty is to God, so are we willing to sacrifice for the sake of the Kingdom? This kind of obedience will often put us in a counterpoint position to the dominant ethos of the institutions of which we are a part. And this may well involve walking the way of the cross.

Call to the unfamiliar
Nudged by the troubling Spirit

I am very much a person of the familiar places. And as such, I have revisited many times historic Franeker, the town of my boyhood years. The subsequent places where I have lived and moved away from continue to be the places that powerfully draw me. I love to walk their streets again and remember with gratitude and pain the years that I spent there.

These familiar places are not simply out there, they are also part of the very fabric of my being. Place becomes a part of one's psyche. One's inner world is shaped by the context and experiences of the outer world.

But I have also been drawn to unfamiliar places and so far have lived in Europe, Australia, Asia and North America. But I am a reluctant wanderer: change and transitions are difficult for me.

The spiritual journey is, in one sense, no different from what I have described above. It too has its familiar places and its mysteries.

Merton notes that 'the true solitary... has been called out of what was familiar to him in order to seek strangely and painfully after what he knows not what'.[90]

While the monk lives in the sedately familiar world of the monastic community, and with the vow of stability has made that his place, that cannot be his only place no matter how wonderful that community of faith may be.

It matters little whether we are monks, business executives or artists, our whole lives cannot revolve around where we live and what we do.

At least we cannot live like that if we are involved in the spiritual quest. For out of the security of who we are, where we live and what we do, we are always called to a strange and haunting dissonance. To a not-having in our having. To a not-knowing in the midst of our wisdom.

In the midst of our world of work and play, we are nudged by the troubling Spirit who is not an evil spirit but God's creative Spirit. Stirring. Gently agitating. Ruffling the surfaces of our settled and secure existence.

The issue here is not so much the nudge to move elsewhere, but the challenge to be free in what we do and where we are so that these things don't possess us.

In this, we are called both upward and outward. We are called to be closer to the heart of God which is the mystery of faith in order to be more present to the neighbour who bears the marks of the hidden Christ.

Thus while we are thankful for all that is part of our settled world, we are also called to transcend our familiar world.

And in this, we need to learn the art of detachment. This is the first movement of the true solitary. Through detachment, one moves to emptiness, and in the emptiness one is found by God to see and experience life more truly from God's perspective.

Detachment never begins in certainty, but only in faith. It starts in darkness, but leads to the hidden God who makes his way known.

Is having faith good for us?
Engaging all of life

There is an uneasy tension that runs through the history of the West. This tension can be symbolized in the differences between the Renaissance and the Reformation. But its roots go back to the much older question whether Athens and Jerusalem have anything to do with each other. Or to put all of that in much more contemporary terms: does a focus on human ability, creativity and culture have anything to do with a life of faith and prayer.

Responses to this fundamental issue are many and varied. There are certainly those who believe that to be spiritual means a withdrawal from the world. This attitude was an aspect of the iconoclasm that left many churches across Europe with plain glass windows as a replacement for the broken beautiful stained glass windows with their pictorial representation of the gospels.

At the opposite end of the continuum, there are those who claim that a life of faith is bad and dangerous for it blinds us to the realities and needs of our world. The Marxist concept of religion as an opiate is a not too distant modern notion.

Merton suggests to us that 'reliance on God...does not mean passivity. On the contrary it liberates man for a clearly defined activity, "the will of God".'[91] This helps us part way in that it is good to be reminded that one's relationship with God does not mean self-negation. Life with God makes us more fully human as we live in harmony with our creator and redeemer. A life of faith and prayer is, therefore, an invitation to a fuller life, not an emasculated one. This is truly good news!

But what needs to be further probed is the idea of being liberated to do the will of God.

The key idea here is that to do what God wants is good rather than bad for us. This is not a relationship of back-breaking servitude, but one of joining with God in love and freedom to see the purposes of God further manifested in our beautiful but broken world. While God's authority is fully acknowledged, this is a relationship of partnership. You are my friends, Jesus said to his disciples.

But what is the will of God and does that include building society as well as the Church, art as well as prayer, business as well as social justice? The answer is clearly, yes!

While there is a deeply counter-cultural dimension to biblical Christianity rooted in the idea that all of life is not what comes our way here because there is an eschatological future, the Bible celebrates all of life. Work, family, sexuality, creativity, productivity, governance and every facet of life is to be lived to the full, to the glory of God and the blessing of the neighbour.

Thus faith and prayer should not sideline us to a narrow corridor of life. In fact, it places us in wide open spaces. It invites us into all the fray of life, but from a godly centre and with a godly vision that seeks the values of God's reign rather than the values of our own human self-determination and self-sufficiency.

To live without faith and prayer is to be cast adrift. To live with faith and prayer is to be anchored even though the storms of life may blow.

Discouragement
Finding the resources to do good

The idea that we can breeze through life, with always favourable winds, is a myth that comes from a culture that is blindly optimistic and unfortunately unrealistic.

To follow this analogy further: there are also times of life-threatening storms and the pathetic doldrums where the winds have gone into hibernation.

Life, seemingly indiscriminate, has a way of giving easy blessings and difficult and painful lessons. Gain and loss, joy and despair and progress and regression seem to be our common lot. And there seems to be no biased selection of candidates. All, irrespective of race, status and gender, experience life's mixed blessings. This, of course, is not to suggest that because of systemic oppression and injustice some don't experience life's mixed blessings with greater pain and severity.

Now it is hardly surprising that many of us will attempt to do things that guard us from life's seeming irrationality and unpredictability. The urban surge is itself a move away from a more vulnerable rural lifestyle subject to the forces of nature.

But there are many other indicators. Insurance. Retreatism. Community. Religion. The list is endless in our attempts to make life more tolerable and manageable.

And so we should! There is no virtue in passive resignation. There is no reason why we should not do all in our power to make life as liveable as possible and to stem the forces of chaos and evil that continue to threaten our existence.

But no matter how hard we try and to what extent we continue to explore and implement our technological capabilities, control and success elude us. Moreover, our very solutions seem to bring in their wake further problems and greater anxiety. Our technology threatens nature. Our nuclear capabilities threaten our world. And some genetic experiments seem to threaten our very humanity.

But finally, the challenge is not control nor is it passive resignation, but a willingness to enter into the mystery of life without fear.

Merton notes that 'because our own resources inevitably fail us, we are all more or less subject to discouragement and to despair'.[92] And one can add to this list: we will all experience pain, misunderstanding, rejection and loneliness.

While we may want to run from these and other difficulties, I suggest we need to embrace and befriend them if we wish to enter life's secrets.

Discouragement can move us to find new resources of faith and hope. Loss can help us to revise what is really worthwhile. Rejection can move us into greater solidarity with the exploited of our time. And death can move us to the ultimate surrender of embracing a life beyond this one.

Christianity encourages us to work for change and transformation in our fallen world. It challenges us to do good in the face of evil. It invites us to hope in the face of despair. But it also calls us to embrace the mystery of life. It draws us to a trusting Job whose faith in God remained unshakeable in the midst of such great loss.

That dangerous word
Hearing Scripture's transformative message

In our therapeutic age many Christians read the Bible for its healing and comforting message. That these are important themes in the Bible needs no further elaboration. But to hold that these are the only themes involves a serious misreading of Scripture.

Scripture is not primarily a book of comfort, but a book with a transformative message. While the Bible brings us words of consolation in times of difficulty, it never wants to leave us where we are, but to move us forward. Even its message of healing is not simply one that makes us feel better, but one that draws us more fully into conformity to Christ.

Thomas Merton notices that in the Bible 'there are religious, ritualistic, priestly elements...(and) prophetic, iconoclastic and anti-establishment trends'.[93] He is right. And even though the priestly elements are there, there is nothing inherently conservative even about those themes. For all the themes of Scripture are cast in the framework of a God who loves generously, redeems holistically and seeks to transform us totally.

But more specifically within the prophetic tradition, there are the powerful themes of obedience, transformation, covenant and justice. God's concern is for the poor and marginalized and he calls the rich and powerful to a repentance that blesses the despised of the earth.

While religion ever slides to the right and to the embrace of conservative ethics and politics, the Bible remains a dangerous book calling us to ongoing conversion. That conversion is not simply the call to abandon our own pathetic and pitiful personal wrongdoing, but also involves a conversion from the social deformities that inhabit our soulscape. The idolatries of our time – control, consumerism, exploitation, militarism, narcissism – need to be expelled from our ways of thinking and acting, as much as the personal wrongdoing of greed, pride, lust and deception.

But at the heart of the biblical prophetic message – and this is what is so deeply disturbing for most of us – there lies the call not only to be holy, but also to be incarnational. In other words, we are called not simply to stop doing certain wrongs, but are called to the praxis of doing what is right. We are called not only to stop exploiting the poor, but to join with them in their struggle for justice.

The prophetic word is never a word that we can control. It is ever a word of exposure that catches us by surprise, for while we may have thought that it was for others, it is first of all a word for us. It's a word that lances the boil. It explodes our rationalizations. It throws light into our shadows. And it draws us into the purposes of the reign of God.

Resistance

Believing and living a different ethic

There are some Christians who believe that resistance should not be part of the Christian's vocabulary. For them, this term has too many political overtones. And since they see Christianity as holding a fundamentally conservative ethic, they believe that this type of language is inappropriate.

It is a curiosity that groups of Christians who hold this position do use the term 'resist' in relation to the devil, but do not see this as having socio-political implications. In other words, there is a personal devil who tempts us to personal sin such as greed or lying. And this devil must be resisted. But there is little understanding regarding the way in which greed operates at the socio-political level leaving Third World nations or particular minority groups of people marginalized and victimized.

I believe that the time has come for Christians to reappropriate more radical language. Due to the fear of appearing to be socialist or communist during the 'cold war' period, many Western Christians dropped the language of radicality. Sadly, it was not only a matter of change of language. It was also a matter of change of values. Many Christians became conservative, middle-class suburbanites. Much of the Church also became isolated from the poor and this facilitated the embrace of a conservative ethic.

I personally fail to see how there can be anything conservative about being a Christian. The new life in Christ causes a deep fissure to appear in previously held values. The gospel reorients us to God's upside-down kingdom. The Spirit breaks into and opens up old patterns of thinking and doing and renews old, tired structures and systems through subversive spiritual renewal.

Thomas Merton believes that 'the monk is essentially someone who takes up a critical attitude towards the world and its structures'.[94] This initially sounds surprising. The monk is hidden and seems irrelevant as far as society is concerned. And yet, there is much truth in Merton's observation. The monk in the quest for union with God, and in a lifestyle of celibacy, poverty, obedience and stability, has broken with many of the values of our contemporary world where control, much-having, independence, self-determination and self-fulfilment are so much the order of the day.

What is true of the monk must also become true of us. This does not mean that we should all become monks. What it does mean, though, is that like the monks we must pursue conformity to Christ, and this will put us on a collision course with the worldliness of the world. As a result, we should not only begin to think differently, but live the divine contrariness of God. Thus in the face of war, we pursue peace. In the place of domination, we seek to live godly servanthood. Instead of the pursuit of self-interest, we build community. And rather than the pursuit of the insatiable desire for much-having, we pursue the path of sharing and accountable stewardship.

The silence of the prophets
The move from speaking to weeping

Anyone who would ever want to typify himself or herself as a prophet is very foolish indeed. Being a prophet is not a career. It is a painful calling. It can never be a self-styled vocation, but a reluctant entering into the purposes of God in such a way that those purposes become the heartbeat and the heart cry of the prophet.

The prophet is the fruit of God's sovereignty and the product of the shaping work of the Spirit in the normal formative realities of life. As such, the prophet is marked for the lonely way and the road of suffering as well as the pathway of revelation and penetrating vision.

While prophets exist in all cultures, in the Christian tradition of both Old and New Testaments, prophets were the spokespersons of God. They made known the ways of God to leaders and people, calling them to a truer and purer faith, a greater ethic of social justice and a new way of understanding the God of present grace and future revelation.

In the history of the Church, prophets have had a most ambivalent status. They have been variously leaders of renewal movements within the life of the Church through to charlatans with their ragtag vision for a new world. This difficult status is partly due to the fact that while one can regulate the role of the pastor, that of the prophet is inherently ambiguous. This is particularly so when the prophet seems to be railing against the very institutions that we are a part of and seek to uphold.

Even though the Reformation wanted to freeze the prophetic task to the New Testament era, the prophetic voice has never been extinguished. Whether we go back to the earlier days of a Chrysostom or a John Hus or to contemporary times in the person of a Bonhoeffer, Romero or Tutu, God's strange spokespersons have emerged in the life of the Church, challenging it to respond more fully to the reign of God and to respond to issues of injustice.

But these voices have been all too few, and the culturally captive Church in the West is too bland to raise many such women and men of passion and vision. With our shallow spirituality and commitment to expediency and pragmatism, we have entered the night of silence.

In one of his poems, Merton prophesies – 'the sun goes down upon the prophets; night is falling and there is no answer'.[95] He is speaking about our time. We lack a cohesive theological vision and a committed ecclesiology. We are uncertain about our faith and lack a passion for witness and service. Nurtured in a religious convenience, we lack direction and conviction. And as such, we have no framework for hearing, let alone for responding, to a prophetic voice.

The silence of the prophet is no blessing. It is God's judgement upon our mediocrity. For when no-one can call us forward and out of ourselves and can call communities of faith to a fuller participation in the reign of God, then we can only be blessed with our blindness and self-preoccupation and so condemn ourselves to a sameness that stultifies and disempowers.

But there is hope when the prophets have stopped speaking but are weeping. Maybe their weeping will become the new heralding cry.

Resisting the powers

Discerning the powers of structural evil

Those of us who live comfortable lives in the First World seldom see the fundamental flaws in our social, economic and political landscape. After all, life is good so why preoccupy oneself with the difficulties of our world. Moreover, what can one person do anyway. So it's better to enjoy what one has rather than being miserable about what others do not have.

Sadly, this ethos has become a part not only of Western individualism and self preoccupation, but also of the Church in the West. The Church has hardly empowered and formed its members to think differently and critically of our world and to live lives with a passion for justice. Conformity and comfortability, rather than a spirituality of dissonance, characterizes the Church.

It hardly needs to be said, however, that things should not be this way. The call to faith calls us into an identification with Jesus Christ and his vision for the Kingdom. Being a part of Christ means becoming a bearer of his Kingdom and continuing Christ's mission in the world. This mission is the repetition of the miracles of reconciliation, forgiveness, peacemaking and healing. This reflects the vision of Christ as the great high priest and our continuing in this priestly activity having become priested through faith in Christ, baptism, participation in the Eucharist and the empowerment of the Spirit.

But we are also invited to follow Christ the prophet who calls for the conversion of the powerful to serve the weak, to bring in the jubilee of God's justice and the shalom of God's kingdom.

That we are more inclined to follow the priestly Christ rather than Christ the prophet comes as no surprise. The former is always more acceptable than the latter. While priests are seen as the healers, prophets are seen as the great disturbers. Yet ironically, prophets are part of the great healing mission of God. Their vision is not simply the transformation of the individual, but the healing communities, the social order and the creation.

The Church needs to recover this vision. Merton reminds us of some of the things that are wrong with our world. He speaks of 'this complacent sorcerer's apprentice who spends billions on weapons of destruction...(and) cannot provide decent meals, shelter and clothing for two thirds of the human race'.[96] More wrongs could be added, including the ongoing exploitation of the Third World by the First World. However, it is not what is wrong with our world that can provide a sustaining motivation for our action.

It is the love and concern of the God of the Bible to bring healing to individuals and peace to communities. It is God's desire for justice and wholeness that should move us to live in and for God's kingdom. And living in the Kingdom provides us with a vision so different from that of our contemporary world. This vision calls us to resist the powers of this age and to pray and work for the blessings of God's reign in our hearts and in our communities.

BEING FOR
The Search for Transformative Action

As the people of God we are not simply in the world to worship God and to care for each other as members of the body of Christ. We are also called to involvement in the world. Love for God must issue in love of neighbour.

One starting point is to recognize that we are very much *in* the world. The natural world and the gifts of culture sustain us. To both, we also need to make our careful contribution. We are called to both the responsible stewardship of creation and the exercise of gifts, skills and abilities which contribute to human and societal well-being.

As a result, Christians may outwork their vocation of being followers of Christ and witnesses to God's kingdom of grace in every sphere of life that brings good to our world. Thus we are encouraged to serve in the fields of science, commerce, the arts, education, politics, social welfare and the many other spheres of human activity and endeavour.

Living a world-formative spirituality, Christians do not turn their faces away from the problems and issues of their time, but immerse themselves in family building, friendship formation, societal participation, the challenges of the marketplace, institution building and the many other activities that sustain and benefit the human community.

But there is a sense in which Christians are not of the world. While fully immersed in the world, they seek to resist the worldliness of the world by rejecting its dominant values when these do not accord with the biblical vision. Thus Christians are always ambivalent. They seek to support the good, but wish to resist the evil in their world and in their own lives.

Thomas Merton as a Trappist monk was not part of an activist religious order which sought to affect directly society through acts of service. He belonged to a contemplative order, and yet he was very much involved in the issues of his day and had a deep concern for his world.

Merton believed that we are never called to a narrow spirituality which has only heavenly things in view and fails to engage us in the beauty and pain of our world. As a writer, he addressed many of the issues of social injustice of his time. But more importantly, Merton provides us with a vision where God and world meet in the incarnation, and where spirituality outworks itself in contemplation and action.

We need to be careful that our engagement in the world is not simply a programmatic one, where we jump onto any and every current social bandwagon. Rather, our engagement should flow out of a double contemplation. On the one hand, we are called to the contemplation of God and his Word. But on the other, we are called to the contemplation of the world, being particularly attentive to its beauty, creativity and innovation while at the same being aware of its propaganda, dysfunctionality and idolatry and its injustice and pain.

What we wish to do is to bring the wisdom of God to our world and the issues of our world to the grace and mercy of God.

Our involvement in the world is not simply the official task of the Church. It's both a personal involvement outworking itself in the places where we live and work as well as a corporate involvement. This means that we work through the Church and its agencies as well as joining hands with community-based organizations to do God's good in our world.

Doing this kind of good involves the task of proclamation, but encompasses much more. Our mission in and to the world is to be holistic. Word and deed. Evangelism and social action. Church planting and societal transformation. Prayer and politics.

The ultimate basis for the call to transformative action is not activism. It springs from the love of God which draws and empowers us and turns our face to the neighbour. Being blessed by God, we seek to bless others. And our concern is not simply to see individuals transformed but also families, neighbourhoods and the institutions of our land.

God's vision for transformation involves our inward dysfunctionality, our relational brokenness, our communal idolatry and our national and international failure to bring peace and justice. Ultimately, the biblical vision is for the restoration of all things and the healing of the nations.

In this grand task, it is God who is the architect and builder. We are invited to join with God's Spirit in the work of renewal.

Spirituality *of everyday life*
Being fully immersed in our world

Thomas Merton once wrote, 'it is in the ordinary duties and labours of life that the Christian can and should develop his spiritual union with God'.[97]

In one sense, these are surprising words from a Trappist monk where so much of life and spirituality are linked to the extraordinary. Celibacy. Poverty. Obedience. Stability. And a life spent in the worship of God, prayer and silence.

Of course, there is more to the life of the Trappist monk. Daily work is also a part of the rhythm of life.

But in another sense, these are understandable words, for they lie at the heart of the biblical message. Since God created and maintains the natural world and in the incarnation revealed himself in Jesus Christ, God's orientation can hardly be regarded as other-worldly. This, of course, is not to say that God and the world are one. They remain distinct. But if God reveals himself *in* the world, then it is there that we can meet with God. God among us. God with us. This means that we can be fully immersed in the world and still know the face of God.

Christians who believe that we need to move away from the world in order to be with God undermine the significance of both the creation and the incarnation.

The heart of living a biblical spirituality has, therefore, nothing to do with a world-denying form of Christianity nor a world-affirming form of spirituality. It has much more to do with living a strange dialectic.

This dialectic has some unusual contours. One is that God can be found or we can be found by God everywhere and not only in the usual religious places. This means the workplace as much as the sanctuary. The body as much as the soul. The crowd as much as the solitary place. It also means that God is often found in the most unlikely places. The streets. Among the poor. In the lives of those with disabilities. In times of crisis. In the boardroom.

The other element of this dialectic is that spirituality is a renewable reality. While we create dogmas, creeds, religious institutions, modes of worship and systems of ethics, none of these in and of themselves can contain the mystery of God and the mystery of faith unless God chooses to be there. In that sense, God is far more elusive than we are inclined to think. And just as well, for religious forms of control are among the most binding and damaging. What all of this may well mean is that when we have found it (our spiritual answers!) we may well have lost it. But when we are seeking, coming in humility and openness, we may well find the great treasure: life in the presence and companionship of God.

While some may be inclined to place scant value on this, it is finding true riches. For being with God and seeing the signs of his presence in our world and serving his kingdom of righteousness and peace, gives us a centre to all that we do whether that be urban design, art, philosophy, philanthropy or the more obvious vocation of religious service.

Facing imperfection
Finding courage to face our broken world

It comes slowly, but once it has arrived it carries the clout of a runaway bus. I am talking about the awakening that our world is far from perfect and that those we have looked up to, respected and trusted are less than what we had first thought. It is a sobering and bloodying experience to realize that such people's feet are made of clay.

While our experience of this may occur with parents, teachers or other significant adult figures in our childhood or teenage years, this rude ripping away of our idealism sooner or later moves to include the Church and other Christian institutions. It may in time become the howling wind that also shakes our understanding of God and rocks the foundations of our faith.

Merton rightly believes that this is inevitable and suggests that this is 'the sacrifice that is demanded of adult men and women: the realistic acceptance of imperfection and of deficiency in themselves, in others and in their most cherished institutions'.[98]

This journey from a naive idealism to a sober realism is difficult, painful and sometimes downright dangerous because it can so easily lead to an unspoken despair or a raging cynicism. None of us enjoys being denuded. And to have our favourite people cut down to size and to have our cherished beliefs overturned seems to threaten us far more than we may have first realized.

But it happens. And more importantly, it needs to happen. It is part of joining the adult world and moving from a Sunday school faith to a more mature faith.

One of the difficulties in this transitional process is that we tend to see the imperfections in others long before we see them in ourselves. As a result, we feed our arrogance, jeopardize relationships and abandon institutional commitments.

Our contemporary context reinforces these observations in that many people are exiting the Church because it fails to meet their expectations and needs. When the Church is seen as the provider of religious services, and we are seen as mere recipients, then this commercial arrangement can easily break down and we go shopping elsewhere.

The sobering of our faith and our experience of life and its institutions, including the Church, need not bring us to a place where we throw the baby out with the bathwater. True faith is a tested faith that has faced the probing questions of doubt.

But true faith is also a humble faith that has dared to look inward in order to uncover and face the demons within. It is a faith that acknowledges our own weakness and fragility and our sheer dependency on the grace of God. Such a faith becomes a tolerant faith. Not tolerant regarding the changes that are needed in our lives, the Church and the world, but a faith that joins hands with others on the road to renewal rather that a faith that blindly blames others for their failures.

A mature faith can face the hard journey in hope and love towards personal and institutional change without demanding instant solutions. Such a faith continues to look to God's persistent involvement in our lives and world. Empowered by the God who journeys with us, we may pray and work even when little seems to change.

Justice and beauty
Recovering a vision for a better world

I have seen it again and again and I am appalled by the way some Christians think that they should outwork their commitment to simplicity and justice.

To live simply and to live with and on behalf of the poor does not mean that one should live in a grungy way.

To live with simplicity for the sake of identification as a reflection of the gospel's concern for the poor does not mean living without beauty. It means, instead, to live with simple beauty rather than with expensive or ostentatious beauty.

In making our cause with the poor, we need to be careful that we do not impose on ourselves an uncompromising asceticism that reflects more a commitment to a certain ideology than a commitment to the gospel and to the following of Jesus.

While it is evident that Jesus identified himself with the poor and the social outcasts of his day, he made room in his life for contact with all sorts of people. And while the Jesus band was supported by others to fulfil their itinerant mission, there is no sense that their lives were characterized by an austere skimpiness. After all, Jesus' outer garment was hardly picked up at St Vincent de Paul – a second-hand clothes shop!

Those of us who are committed to justice issues, work with the poor, and the difficult work of advocacy, and who seek to do this work in concert with rather than removed from the poor, need to be careful that we don't attempt to be more demanding than the gospel and that we don't imbibe the values of a culture of poverty.

There is nothing virtuous about poverty. Poverty is ugly. It dehumanizes and defaces the image of God in people. Poverty feeds resignation as people continue to experience powerlessness. And poverty mars the beauty of the social world that God has given for our habitat.

Here the culture of poverty must be resisted, including the faulty idea that the more we become like the poor the more spiritual we will become and the more effective our ministry will be.

Thomas Merton makes the personal observation: 'I don't really like to get my feet wet, but does that mean that the only way for me to be a saint is to have only one pair of shoes full of holes?'[99]

The negative answer to this question is self-evident. We don't win favour with God in this way and true spirituality is not formed out of this kind of negation.

Simplicity in the service of justice can be marked with celebration, joy and beauty. For in the work of justice we do not respond simply to need, but to the fullness of God's shalom.

Justice reflects the fullness of God's will for us. That fullness is both spiritual and material. It has to do with prayer and economics and with beauty and sacrifice.

Communities of justice, therefore, as signposts of the Kingdom, are called to reflect not only the power of God's reconciliation and peace, but also the generosity of God eschatologically symbolized in the marriage supper of the Lamb.

The unexpected extra
Empowered in loving service

It is not for nothing that the Gospels encourage us to become like little children. This, of course, has nothing to do with becoming childish, but with being child-like. While some may want to emphasize the trusting and compliancy features of childlikeness, I want to stress the sense of wonder that accompanies this phase of life.

I still have many memories as a pre-teenage boy lying flat on my face in the grass watching ants and many of God's other smallest of creatures. What an amazing sub-world with all its activity and beauty! I can still remember the sense of wonderment when I took time to stop and to see and to gaze at the beauty of nature.

The sense of wonder can leave us as we grow older and particularly as we turn our gaze more and more to the social world that we are creating. Instead of wonderment, we so often are left with a sense of competition, alienation, fear and distrust.

Yet it is not only nature that calls us to gaze upon it with the eyes of love and appreciation, the world that we are making, with its art, music, culture and philosophies, also calls us to celebrate and be thankful. For so much is good, even though sometimes so much good is diverted to wrong ends. This occurs particularly when the good leads to the exultation of the self rather than the worship of God, the ultimate giver.

But, however good and broken our world may be, we are called to respond not in fear and cynicism, but in love and hope. This is particularly so when we seek to reach out to others who are in deep need and trouble.

If we see a person *merely* as a street kid, drug addict, young offender, prostitute or troublemaker, then we are insulting the image of God in that person. More specifically, we are allowing that person's difficulties to define their whole being. And as a result, we will often respond in less than fully loving ways.

Here we are also called to wonderment. This person once nestled at a mother's breast, knew something of human care and grew up with blessings. What went wrong? Where are the telling wounds that sent this young person onto destructive pathways? And at the same time, there is the wonderment of God's mystery. What does God desire for this person? And how can I respond and cooperate with God's redeeming and reconstructing intention?

To wonder is to love and hope. This is the magic of the genesis. It is seeing beyond the problem to the redemption, beyond the pain to the healing, beyond the grubby outward appearance to the innermost heart.

When we go from this visionary beginning to practical helping and healing strategies, we encounter the often long and difficult helping road, not without its discouragement and uncertainties. And yet, it is here that we so often find extra grace.

Merton notes, 'sometimes you get the feeling that when you are carried away by this desire of love for souls, God is beginning to pour out everything upon you, to deluge you with all that you need, to overwhelm you with spiritual or even temporal favours'.[100]

This is true. In serving the poor and needy we are often graciously empowered. Extra grace is often the surprise. It's as if God is bending over us with benediction and generosity when we serve the little ones who are in such distress.

In this experience we realize anew that in faithful giving, God so graciously outgives us.

Spirituality and service
Action nurtured by God's embrace

There are those who foolishly try to separate spirituality and service and contemplation and action as if the two have nothing to do with each other. The practice of solitude, so they claim, and the work for justice are at opposite ends of the spectrum. After all, aren't there religious orders that withdraw from the world and those that actively serve in education, urban mission and community development? And aren't there Christians who are especially good at praying while others get their hands dirty and get the job done?

Well, yes, that is somewhat true. But the distinctions are too crudely drawn. Things are not as clearly packaged as we Westerners tend to believe. Life and spirituality are to be much more integrated.

Merton is adamant that 'we cannot live for others until we have entered this solitude'.[101] He is right. The work of service can only come out of and be sustained by a deep spirituality. And those who violate this simple dictum do so at cost to themselves.

Fifteen years on the streets involved in inner-city mission with all the frustrations and difficulties, and all the joys of seeing transformation in the face of overwhelming odds, has taught me that if one doesn't pray and draw close to God one will never sustain the journey.

Let me try to explain why that is so.

One of the first risks in service and social justice ministries is that we can begin to believe too much in what we are doing. Too much of our persona becomes embedded in our activity.

When things go well, we are buoyant and confident. When we face the demons of structural evil we easily become discouraged or disillusioned.

In other words, we are too much a part of and too close to what we do and we almost don't have an identity or a life apart from the good work we are doing.

The obvious risk is that it becomes too much our work. And with that come all sorts of problems including our inability to delegate, empower others and remain truly dependent on God's Spirit and grace.

A further risk has to do with the motivational centre of our activity. We can so easily tap into forms of control and power that begin to negate a walk of humility and the need to minister out of weakness.

The practice of solitude allows us to distance ourselves from the work of our hands. It draws us away from giving to receiving. From action to prayer. From people to God. From difficulties to quiet hope. From pain to the healing presence of God.

In solitude, where we seek God in spirit and truth, we discover the true centre of who we are and all that we do. We discover that we are sons and daughters of God and so we welcome others to God's banquet. We are reminded that we are embraced in Christ who loves us for who we are rather than what we do, and so we serve out of thankfulness and joy. In solitude we rediscover the power of prayer and the galvanizing dynamism of hope, and so we serve having been blessed by the God who welcomes us home and calls us onto the dusty road.

Working for change
Call to discernment and partnership

Having been an activist for most of my life, I am now no longer sure whether the concept of working for change is the only way to put it and is the full picture.

The phrase, of course, sounds great. It has a heroic ring about it. It implies that the actors have an understanding of what is wrong with our society and how it can move to embrace the vision of the new. Implicit in the phrase is also the idea that one has the means to get from where we are to where we ought to be.

All of this, in my opinion, is far too pretentious and triumphalistic.

My experience of working for change is that it is a far more fragile and vulnerable endeavour. One can see something of the local need, but the global realities that impact and help to shape these difficulties often remain hidden or vague. One can begin to do something, but remain unsure whether this is a good starting point or insertion into the need. One can be well under way in the execution of certain change strategies and meet with totally unexpected opposition and resistance. And of course, the worst case scenario is that at the end of the day a lot of energy and resources have been utilized, but nothing much has changed, or things may have gone backwards.

Merton is, therefore, right in alluding to the vulnerable nature of these endeavours: 'a radical change that goes with genuine renewal implies a certain anguish, insecurity and risk'.[102]

In the light of the above, I wonder whether it is better to talk of working *with* change rather than simply *for* change.

What I have in mind here is not to undermine human initiative and endeavour, but the need to see ourselves as part of a much bigger picture. The issue is not simply what we are doing, it is what we are doing in concert with others. Effective strategies for change all have to do with the practice of partnership.

Work for change has its genesis in the realization that something is wrong, ineffective, unjust and unacceptable. While we personally may be the victims of this wrong and this galvanizes us into action, we may also simply join in the cause of those who are wronged. Thus we voluntarily enter their pain, cause and struggle.

But what is wrong requires careful discernment, for we are often part of the wrong. It is also so easy to generalize and to victimize and to create false bogeymen. It is so easy to be simplistic and reactionary. And therefore we need both spiritual discernment and the wisdom of others.

The development and implementation of effective change strategies requires mobilizing others. Here again is the need for cooperation and partnership.

While we may want to be the sole prophet calling for change, we need to see where the creative Spirit is hovering. And we need to discern where people are crying and praying, where others are moving and acting, where signs of hope are appearing in a landscape of indifference and where we find the courage and company to move forward.

Daily work

Cooperating with our creator God

We sometimes think that the life of a monk is a complete oddity and that it has no relevance for the real world. What is biased about this view is that it makes the monk's life of worship and prayer irrelevant, which of course, it can never be. To pray on behalf of our broken world is an important service indeed!

But monks not only pray. They also work. And work is not seen as an aberration in the rhythm of their communal life. Nor is it seen as a sideline to their spiritual activities. Work is not an interruption, but an expression of their life of faith before God. Merton writes, 'also in manual labour we become helpers and cooperators with God the creator and administrator of the world – we become instruments of his divine providence – we help him change and renew the face of the earth'.[103]

As laypersons working in the marketplace we can take these words to heart. Ordinary work can be a sacred duty. Work is not simply facilitating our career path. It is not only a matter of status in our world. Nor is it simply a matter of earning enough to sustain our existence.

Work, whether in the rural, industrial, human services or information technology areas, can be a way of serving God through serving the wider community.

I have had the joy of working not only in formal Christian ministries, but also in secular employment. I regard the latter as much a ministry as the former, and in some ways secular work was more of a challenge. This was through not only seeking to be a Christian witness in the workplace, but seeking to do God's good there as well.

We work in a business or for a company to use and maximize our gifts and talents. We want the company to provide good products and services and therefore we want the company to succeed, even though we may be only employees. And we want the company to have a social conscience and to be motivated by more than mere profit-making.

To be a worker is part of God's intention for our life. In doing good work we not only sustain and express ourselves, but we also provide products and services which benefit others. And in doing this, we help build the human community.

The Christian is always called to a double task: to build the human community as well as the community of faith. In doing both, we glorify God as creator and redeemer.

Being and doing
Finding a holistic approach to life

I grew up in a setting where doing was the first and the last word. Little wonder that I developed the notion that I was loved for what I did, not for who I was. Sadly, this governed my life for a long time. I became the activist and the achiever who often pushed himself harder than anyone else.

Surprisingly my Christian conversion did not automatically change this faulty set of motivations. In fact, things only became worse. I became an activist in ministry and a compulsive do-gooder.

It was only later through the attentive love of my wife, children and friends that my orientation began to change. Their love had nothing to do with my performance. In fact, they loved me in my failure, weakness and vulnerability. In my subsequent journey, I have experienced the sheer audacity of God's beneficent love through friends who have cared for me and encouraged me in the midst of struggles despite the public persona of ability and having it all together.

Merton makes the comment that 'the monk is important more for what he is than for what he does'. This is true, in fact, of every Christian. 'Being' always takes precedence over '"doing" and "having"'.[104]

All of this has to do not only with the benefits we receive from the healing presence of others, but also with an understanding of the sheer magic of the grace of God. God loved us while we were enemies, while we were strangers, while we were hell-bent on the pursuit of our own stupidities. The Hound of Heaven pursued us in our stubbornness. The forgiving grace of Christ cleansed us from our folly and sin. And the father and mother heart of God welcomed us home, succouring and sheltering us in the trembling experience of welcome and hospitality rather than rejection and exile.

Having been embraced and affirmed by the God of all mercy and having found my place in a family of nurture and care and in the community of faith which continues to proclaim God's good news to me, I am empowered to act and to do God's good in our fragile and wounded world.

Duty

The persistent practice of responsibility

I must confess that I easily get bored with what I am doing, particularly if I think I have mastered it, which, of course, is often not the case. And so I want to move on to some new challenging project and embark on a new adventure.

At this stage of my life's journey, I am still not at all sure whether this constitutes some flaw in my make-up or whether it is a blessing in disguise. Maybe it simply highlights the fact that there are blessings in our weakness and failings in our strength.

But in spite of these tendencies, life soon taught me that its most basic rhythm is not creativity, but maintenance. The daily pattern of life is not running from one exciting new project to another, let alone from one relationship to another. Such a compulsive drivenness reflects one's inability to celebrate the ordinary and to be thankful for what has been given.

Life is to be lived differently from this. It has everything to do with the persistent practice of responsibility. There are the simple daily duties of running our households. The need to care for family members. The challenge to faithfulness in our jobs, which are so often repetitive and at worst boring. There are responsibilities that we have assumed for neighbours and friends and our brothers and sisters in the community of faith to which we belong.

Merton makes the helpful comment, 'duty does not have to be dull. Love can make it beautiful and fill it with life.'[105] He is not only right, but we could go further and say that true love can express itself in duty. If it doesn't, love may well remain a fleeting sentiment.

While love may be the raging or quiet and meandering stream, duty is the river bank that gives love its focus and direction. Duty, therefore, done gladly and in order to serve the other, gives love its concrete and practical expression.

In a world that places so much value on our occupational status, it is important to learn the art of doing very ordinary things. The performance of ordinary duties can not only humanize us, but also mould us for service in the kingdom of God.

Obedience
Expressing a heart full of love

I do not want to suggest that only the communities of faith in the Third World are living in fidelity to the gospel and that the Churches in the First World are not, but I do see some persistent and deep-seated problems in the Churches in the Western world.

One of these problems is that First World Christians seem largely to have lost the idea that a living faith involves a life of obedience.

Many Third World Christians with little resources and infra-structure live a life of faith, obedience and costly service. It seems that many First World Christians, who materially have so much, are stingy in their service and ambivalent about a life of discipleship and commitment.

I believe that at this point, First World Christians are demon-strating the extent to which they have become captive to major themes in contemporary culture. In a world that emphasizes self-fulfilment, costly service and relinquishment don't quite fit. When freedom is lauded, obedience can easily be misunderstood. Where individualism is championed, concern for the neighbour can easily fall into disrepair.

Strangely, in a culture that already has so much, we find an inability to set limits. We ever want more, and seem to be forever complaining that enough is not enough.

In this setting, obedience is a ready casualty. The life of faith, sadly, seems to be more about what we can get rather than how we live in gratitude, obedience and faithful service.

Monks do know something about obedience and maybe can help point the way. They live in obedience to the Word of God, and to the leadership and vision of their community. But while they have made formal commitments, obedience is ultimately a matter of the heart. Merton notes that 'obedience must be rediscovered, not as submission to legalistic authority, but as openness to the hidden will of God'.[106]

While obedience always involves a careful and joyful listening to Scripture and includes listening to our spiritual mentors and guides, including the pastoral authorities in the community of faith in which we participate, obedience is ultimately the bending of the ear to the heartbeat of God.

It is also bending the heart to the voice of God. It is attuning ourselves to the orchestrations of the Spirit.

Obedience ultimately cannot spring from the demands of external authorities. It can only spring from a heart set free and full of love. Obedience comes from the captivated heart, entranced by the generosity of the God of all grace who calls us to respond to others in the same way as God has blessed us.

Thus a deepening of obedience does not spring from a harping asking and demanding, but from a deeper enchantment with the grace and the way and purpose of God.

Such obedience is a renewable and fragile mystery, rather than a once-for-all certainty. It is therefore the gift that must be found again and again.

Action and contemplation
A holistic approach to life and ministry

Merton was a contemplative. He lived the life of a Trappist monk observing silence, the liturgical cycle, prayer and contemplation and daily work. He was not part of an apostolic order involved in the world through the ministries of evangelism, teaching or social concern.

I am an activist. I have never lived in a monastery. I have lived life in the world working in industry, a government department and in a university setting and I have been involved in pastoral work, community work and teaching.

Our worlds are even farther apart than what appears from the above. Merton is a Roman Catholic. I am an uneasy Protestant – uneasy not because I am thinking of converting, but because I fear that we Protestants have thrown too much of the baby out with the bathwater. And there are many other ways in which we are so different.

Yet, we have a lot in common. Merton the contemplative engaged the issues of his time. He was outspoken about political and social justice issues. He raised his voice in the marketplace, even though he was in the place of prayer.

I, on the other hand, was in the marketplace and needed to learn to raise my voice to heaven.

Merton tells us that 'action is charity looking outward to other men, and contemplation is charity drawn inward to its own divine source. Action is the stream and contemplation is the spring.'[107]

We all need to learn this basic rhythm of life wherever we may find ourselves and whatever our vocation. Activism can never be sustained without prayer, for we need the gift of perseverance as we seek to do good in our refractory world. The work of evangelism and justice is never easy, particularly not since we have to face and challenge the powers of our age.

But activism should not only be sustained by prayer. It also should be born out of prayer. In prayer we listen to God's heartbeat and seek his will. In prayer we commit ourselves to do God's bidding, no matter how difficult or challenging that may be. And in prayer we seek the specifics of our action in the world.

In the to and fro movement of prayer and action we can be sustained, and our activity can be sustained because we seek God's participation and empowerment.

Spirituality in a secular world
The hidden life of prayer

We all too readily develop our neat little categories, put people into particular boxes and overdraw distinctions and thereby undermine life's complexity and subvert the possibility of a more holistic approach to life. And so we make our distinctions between those called to a secular vocation and those called to a sacred one. Not only do we distinguish clergy and laity, but we also distinguish between lay involvement in medicine, social welfare and teaching and those working in the field of commerce and industry. The one is somehow judged as being more worthy than the other.

An all too ready distinction that we make is between the monk who lives a life of prayer and the layperson who lives a life of work. Yet, these neat categories need to be challenged.

Merton makes the observation, 'far from being exempted from service in the battles of his age, the monk, as a soldier of Christ, is appointed to fight these battles on a spiritual, hidden front – in mystery – by prayer and self-sacrifice'.[108] Simply put, the monk with his face turned towards God still has his face turned towards the world. Being in a monastery, the monk has left the world, but has not abandoned it. For in the life of solitude, humility, obedience, prayer and contemplation, the monk embraces concern for the world as much as he seeks to embrace the heart of God.

The converse should also be true. We who live in the world, and are called to marriage, family, neighbourliness and a life of work in agriculture, industry, the arts or government, should embrace the disciplines of solitude, prayer and contemplation.

While the monk runs the risk of being so heavenly-minded that he is no earthly good, we laypersons run the risk of being so engrossed in the daily affairs of life that we have lost the ability to hear God's heartbeat, to seek his will and to pray on behalf of our world.

We who serve God in the marketplace need to become contemplatives in the midst of life. We are never simply workers. We are first of all called to be worshippers and prayers.

From our own woundedness
Ministry and the places of pain

My church traditions – I have intimately experienced several – never taught me anything about the link between ministry and vulnerability. The one tradition stressed relying on the Word of God together with good training leading to competence. The other stressed openness to the Spirit of God and made a link between effectiveness and spiritual power.

In the one tradition, I was a conduit for the Word. In the other, I was a channel of the Spirit. But in both, I was part of the excluded middle. It did not seem to matter so much where I was at as long as I functioned effectively.

I believe that this is a defective view of how God works. While I am not suggesting that ministry simply depends on us, since it is God's grace, healing and power that is key to any situation, we are part of the equation. And where we are at has something to do with the way we function.

Merton makes the observation that 'once you have experienced the pain of your own infirmity... you soon learn compassion and a corresponding tenderness toward other people'.[109] He is writing out of the pain of many wasted years before he found his vocation as a monk.

Most of us can write our own script at this point. There are things that have happened that have humbled us and made us less messianic, not so full of ready-made answers, and more aware of our own lack of wholeness.

Rather than these things being a handicap to effective ministry, they are blessings in disguise. For if we 'possess' the Word and the Spirit, but have no love, sensitivity, gentle ways in connecting up with others, willingness to be open to their heart cry and willing to be vulnerable ourselves, then we may not be as effective as we think.

If we think that ministry can only come out of strength, we may have to do a major rethink. Ministry can also come out of our own brokenness. This is not to say that we can minister out of our disappointment, frustration and anger. But we can serve out of our vulnerability. For in that place, we will be all the more dependent on God and sensitive to the other person.

Doing and surrendering
Recognizing our part and God's part

The life of faith and that of responsibility are not two separate worlds. In other words, I shouldn't just believe and do nothing, nor should I do everything and leave God out of the picture. These two worlds should interpenetrate. But how they do, is always a bit of a mystery.

This does not mean that it automatically follows that if I do my part, God will do his. Life is simply not like that. For often, God will do something unexpected when we haven't even thought about it, let alone anticipated it or contributed towards it. The God of surprises does not dance to our tune nor does God simply respond to our initiatives. The Sovereign Lord works in his own mysterious way his wonders to perform.

Nevertheless, faith and responsibility, prayer and action, trust in God and human initiative are part of the exhilarating kaleidoscope of life. And we should welcome God's participation as much as God welcomes ours. After all, we are made in God's image and God has given us a task to do. We are vice-regents under God's Lordship in this challenging but broken world of ours.

Merton, in pursuing acceptance into the monastery, writes, 'I had done everything that was in my power, the rest was in . . . [God's] hands.'[110]

We all have had these exciting and scary moments. We have committed ourselves to a friendship, but we need to hear from the other person. We have applied to do a university course, but need to hear from the scholarship committee. The situations are myriad.

And so we wait, praying and trusting that we have been moving in the right direction for our lives. We believe that God was also with us in the genesis of the direction as well as in its unfolding. And so we trust that everything will fall into place.

It often does! But not always! Sometimes the expected open door is firmly shut in our face. We are disappointed. We may even question everything. But finally we have to move on. And when we find the grace to do this, it means that we have truly prayed: Lord I commit this situation into your hands.

The Other

Welcoming people in Christ's name

I have met very pious Christians as well as very worldly ones. I know that I am supposed to respect the former more than the latter. But often I don't.

This has nothing to do with wanting to condone worldliness. I believe that Christians transformed by the grace of Christ should demonstrate a lifestyle that is qualitatively different. Rather, it has to do with my reaction to a spirituality that often is narrow and bigoted and that believes itself to be so virtuous that it looks down on other people.

I believe that we are to be neither pious nor worldly, but Christlike in our attitude and approach to others, including those who are not of our faith. And being Christlike has something to do with welcoming people rather than judging or condemning them, particularly when their lives are already so vulnerable and distraught.

Much of our lives, Rita, my wife, and I have worked with marginalized people. These included people with a criminal record, drug addicts, young people living on the streets and men and women in prostitution. We soon discovered that when treated with respect and when welcomed into our home and lives, these young people not only opened up about their hurt and pain, but many stayed long enough to find new life in Christ and a new direction for their lives.

Merton makes the observation that 'if we meet the non-Christian as a brother we meet him on ground that is Christian'.[111]

Sadly, and at worst, we so often meet the other with our judgement, or at best with our sermonettes. Instead, we should see people, no matter how twisted their lives may be, as made in God's image and therefore as people of dignity and worth. In welcoming them, we provide the beginnings of a safe place where they can begin to process their anger and pain. And in joining with them in their journey of recovery, we become signs of hope for them.

I believe that we should see people much more through the eyes of faith than with the measure of careful calculation. Rather than seeing their sin, we should see their potential in Christ. And rather than concentrating on their strange behaviour or reactions, we should encourage them to face and seek healing for their pain. In this, we become the signposts of God's love for those who have lost their way.

It's unfair
Living in an unjust and broken world

I do know something of growing up in a world without privilege – a migrant kid in one of Brisbane's poorer suburbs. I also know the challenge of literally having to pray for the next meal during the early days of establishing a ministry among drug addicts and prostitutes. And now, many decades later, I know the insecurity of not having one permanent place in which to live.

But I have nothing to complain about. I have never experienced hunger and many blessings have come my way. My worst form of suffering has been to stare in the face of others who are suffering.

Merton writes, 'the world is terrible, people are starving to death and freezing and going to hell with despair and here I sit with a silver spoon in my mouth and write books?'[112]

I share Merton's sentiments. I have worked for many years with homeless and troubled young people and have experienced close at hand the poverty of others. But I have never fully been a part of their lives even though I sought to help and bless.

I never felt good about any of this, neither their poverty and pain, my helping, nor my privileges.

But I never had the courage fully to join the most marginalized and become one of them. I reluctantly believed that serving them and journeying with them was the best thing to do.

This has left me with a profound sense of unease and the never-ending question, why them and why not me? They are no less deserving of a decent life and I am no more deserving.

All of this becomes even more complicated when the poor are members of the community of faith and are brothers and sisters in Christ. Jesus has also given them the gift of abundant life, yet why are they experiencing life so differently?

And so while the poor live with the pain of suffering and lack of opportunity, I live with a pain arising from guilt and helplessness. And this pain goes on and on in our world lacking justice and full of people like me who try to do something, but never enough.

Haste

Dealing with our compulsions

It is no surprise that the earlier dream of a leisure society in the First World has not materialized. Many of those in employment are working longer hours than ever before, while others spend their time queuing for jobs that attract hundreds of applicants. At the same time, technology has made many aspects of our lives easier, and retirees, if they have the financial resources, can tap into the leisure dream.

But life does not seem to have slowed down. We are busier than ever and much of life is lived at a hectic pace. This is particularly true of urban dwellers whether in the West or in the Third World.

And like others, Christians are caught in a great juggling act between work, family, church and societal responsibilities, with seemingly never enough time for everything. Consequently, our lifestyle seems to have a freneticism about it. Time for haste! But little time for solitude and reflection!

It is somewhat of a surprise to learn that this problem has even penetrated the sacred walls of the monastery. Merton, the Trappist monk, living a life of worship, work, prayer and contemplation, admits: 'my haste is just as immoral as anybody else's and comes from the same selfish desire to get quick results with a small amount of effort'.[113]

The problem we are dealing with here is not so much the issue of lack of time, but the reality of our compulsions and drivenness.

For Merton, it was the drive to write another book. For others, it is expanding one's business. For others again, it is building a bigger church. And for many, it is crowding our lives with new adventures, experiences and achievements.

For most of us, enough is not enough since we have no idea what enough looks like. Driven by the capitalist quest for more and greater consumption we have simply bought the dominant values of our age which knows so little of down-scaling, simplicity and downward mobility. Everything must become more, bigger and better.

But I think we have an instinctive feel that more does not necessarily equate to better.

One of the secrets of life and of the spiritual journey is the slow realization that the good and worthwhile things of life come slowly and often with difficulty and therefore require faith, patience and hope.

Sabbath-keeping, in whatever way we may wish to outwork that in our contemporary world, times for solitude and reflection, and seasons of prayer, can so easily be seen as wasting time in our pragmatic and achievement-oriented world. And yet these very spiritual disciplines will shape and impregnate everything else that we say and do.

Thus the issue is not to do more and more, which comes out of a compulsive freneticism, but to do what we should do by way of our responsibilities and to do what we may do in the freedom that God gives us, out of a life of prayer and contemplation.

While prayer and the practice of solitude are ends in themselves in that they deepen our friendship with God and with ourselves, these disciplines of grace will affect the way we make decisions, order our daily lives, do our work and dream our dreams.

The quick road is often not the shortest road. And while haste may continue to feed our social self with all its achievements, God invites us to the slow road of his providential care and grace.

Disarmament

Learning the art of peacemaking

During the decade and a half that I worked on the streets in the inner-city, I certainly saw a fair share of violence. Violence was perpetrated not only by troubled young people, but also by those who are meant to uphold the law. Typifications about 'goodies' and 'baddies' soon blur in the murky underside of urban life.

There were also occasions where I was threatened. And it's no fun to have a knife at one's throat with a semi-deranged young person pouring out a series of threats and nonsensical mumbo-jumbo fed by the toxic chemicals that promise utopia, but frequently deliver only the incoherent nightmare.

At such times, I was never afraid. Not so much because I was some sort of hero, but because I had long ago recognized and acknowledged the coward in me.

Not being afraid within a setting of anger, aggression and madness is an important element in the politics of disarmament. For if one is not afraid, one does not need to galvanize oneself into retaliatory action. And this stance is usually picked up by the potential aggressor.

But of course, there could be and should be more to the story. Merton notes that 'true nonviolence...works without aggression, taking the side of the good that it is able to find already present in the adversary'.[114]

Merton is drawing here from the Gospel beatitudes and Gandhi's concept of non-violent resistance. The key idea is that we do not react to a person's paranoia and dysfunctionality, but seek to respond to his or her better and deeper motivations.

This is not easy, and each situation needs to be responded to on its own merits. Concerns for one's own safety should not be factored out of the equation, and no situation of danger should ever be regarded lightly.

The heart of the challenge, however, is for us to become gospel peacemakers in our world. The challenge is to live Francis of Assisi's prayer: make us an instrument of your peace.

Peaceful actions and a peaceful presence can only spring from the purging shaping that makes the peaceful heart. Here our own angers and aggressions and reactions need to be identified, acknowledged and purged.

Some of these angers are the result of our own folly, but some are shaped by our family's biography or our national catastrophes.

As a young boy, I was terribly aggressive and frequently came home with bloodied knuckles. Later I tried to sublimate these aggressive tendencies in sport, then in work and later again in compulsive Christian service.

It was only much later that I came to see how much being a World War II baby had shaped a part of my inner landscape.

So to become peacemakers in our world is not a task that we can undertake without first facing the wars within us. Living in a broken world we ourselves will only add to its brokenness out of our own woundedness. So we first need to come to the Prince of Peace to receive grace, forgiveness and healing. By God's Spirit we need to be purged of the demons within us. And in the face of another's anger or aggression we can only reach out in love as we are empowered by God's presence. Failing this, we will most likely only add to the violence around us.

Good news to the poor
Joining with those who cry for justice

Even though I come from a middle-class family and have held responsible and well-paying vocational positions, I have lived most of my life on the wrong side of the tracks, in poorer neighbourhoods. This was as a result of particular choices. And those were born, not out of necessity, but out of faith and struggle.

Both of these elements were always present. Faith emerged from a reading of the biblical story with its passion for the poor, the stranger and marginalized. Faith was reinforced through a sense of calling. The gentle nudges of the Spirit whispering: this is the way to live, this is the concern of the Father heart of God. But with the shafts of light cast by faith's moments of clarity and inspiration, there were also the spectres of uncertainty and sometimes fear: is this a responsible way to live, particularly with one's children, was a frequent set of concerns.

From these varied, but always precarious journeys of faith, a number of things became, with time, increasingly clear. One matter had to do with self-discovery. The other with the surprising ways of God. The third, with the discovery of the power of the poor in history. And finally, the shocking realization that despite much activity little changes.

Being with the poor always brings with it the invitation to personal transformation. While we come to serve, to help, to encourage, and we seek to do so from a position of strength, we quickly discover that the poor throw light on our own poverty and woundedness. The poor expose our lousy motivations and bring us to the painful realization that we don't have the quick fixes that we thought we had. Thus the poor call us to a painful conversion that touches some of our deepest motivations and expectations.

Living among the poor and joining with them in their journeys of hope and struggle, one becomes much more aware of the surprising presence of God. God is certainly not restricted to the bland safeness of middle-class suburbia – even though behind its closed doors the brokenness of life often plays itself out with volcanic viciousness – God also walks the streets of poverty and despair. Among the poor, the signs of God's grace stand out with greater clarity. In their cry, God's surprising answers are strikingly clear.

One does not need to be with the poor for very long before one discovers an amazing resilience. This is not to suggest that there are no poor without hope and no poor who don't drink themselves to oblivion. But many poor people continue to struggle for life and live in hope even when that hope has been severely tested by the empty promises of politicians and the social welfare system. The poor continue to build family, and to struggle for better education and to move beyond meaningless work.

But serving the poor is no sure march to victory. While some individuals and families may be marginally helped, the majority continue to suffer and struggle. Our world is hardly the domain of justice. We favour the rich and the powerful and barely throw the scraps from our tables to the poor. And our churches are hardly different. Having previously lost its connection to the working classes and the poor, the Church as a predominantly middle-class institution has lost its radical understanding of the gospel. Therefore, we all need to hear again the words of Thomas Merton: 'the Bible is above all the message preached to the poor, the burdened, the oppressed, the underprivileged'.[115]

Doing the will of God
Place of joy, security and purpose

That life cannot be lived against itself is merely stating a simple truism. Life can only be lived meaningfully when we obey the basic 'laws' of life. So if community is a basic reality of life, we can't live meaningfully if we are incapable of being in relationship with others.

There are also other spiritual truisms. One of the most fundamental is that true happiness and purpose is found in knowing and doing the will of God. Or in the words of Thomas Merton, 'freedom can only be found in perfect union and submission to the will of God'.[116]

It is my observation that Christians in the Third World not only believe but also seek to practise this key spiritual dictum. I am less sure about myself and my brothers and sisters in the First World. Living in a culture of complaint and with rising expectations, the idea of the Christian life is much more that God should fit in with our plans and designs rather than the other way round. The basic idea seems to be that we should take care of ourselves, and God will bless us in the process.

As a result of this approach, there seems to be little earnest questing to know, not only the general will of God, but also the more specific will of God for life and service.

It is sad to have one's calling and ministry made fun of by some Christians who think that anything that has to do with self-sacrifice is mere do-goodism at best and sheer irresponsibility at worst.

Against this rather negative view, let me place my own personal testimony. At conversion, I simply assumed that God had the right to direct my life and that my responsibility and joy was wrapped up in the idea that in seeking to do the will of God I would honour God and bless others and that God would also bless me.

While I am not all that sure how much I have honoured God or been a blessing to others, after decades of Christian service I find myself incredibly blessed. There have been companions on the journey. Growth in the midst of pain and difficulty. Opportunities to learn new things. And above all, there has been so much that has enriched my life.

We can't outgive God. When we live in obedience, God will not only use us, but will also nurture us. Thus there is no better place to be than in the will of God.

Effervescent spirituality
Breathing the breath of God

My rather austere Protestant upbringing left me questing for the presence of the Spirit, the ever so seldom mentioned member of the Trinity. Of course, at the time I had no idea that that was what I was looking for. I did not know what I was looking for, only that my hunger for the presence of God was far from satisfied and a gnawing emptiness continued to eat away at the structures and formalities of my faith.

Little wonder! Faith is to be lived in the presence of God; and theological knowledge, churchly participation and acts of service, no matter how important, cannot in themselves, be life-giving. They can only serve as vehicles for the presence of God.

Hunger gives way to prayer, and prayer in its mysterious operation touches the willing hand of God. And from this generous hand the Spirit is given again and again, to renew, enliven and empower.

My experience of the Spirit was both ecstatic and peace-giving. Overwhelming, yet gentle. Powerful, yet beautifying. And since it did not occur within a Pentecostal or Charismatic framework, I had no theological or ecclesiastical language with which to describe, categorize and tame my experience. I was left in the realm of awe and wonder.

But changes were evident, both immediate and long-term. A belief in the miraculous workings of God became a growing conviction. The Spirit's presence became an increasing comfort. An intuitive discernment became a cutting-edge blessing. The experience of spiritual gifts became an empowering reality and a new sense of worship a growing joy.

I was totally surprised to learn that there is a seductive side to all of this.

Merton notes one feature. He writes, 'a burst of spiritual exuberance can tone you up ... but ... when it is all over you may have no more profit than you might have got from a couple of glasses of champagne or a good swim'.[117]

While this comparison hardly does justice to the work of the Spirit, there is an element of truth here, namely, the quest for experience for experience sake. This narcissistic longing of our contemporary age for ever new and exciting experiences. And like bungy jumping, mountain climbing, rapids shooting, it is all in the thrill of the experience.

Many in the Pentecostal and Charismatic movement have exited through the back door after having tasted spiritual thrills in coming through the front door.

But the blessings of the Spirit are not the substance of an effervescent spirituality.

Quite the opposite is the case. The Spirit is given and spiritual gifts are generously imparted to draw us into a faithful following of Jesus who himself lived and served in the power of the Spirit. The Spirit is given not for thrills, but for service to build up the community of faith and to serve powerfully in the world. This service involves proclaiming the gospel of the Kingdom and doing the works of grace and power that transform lives and communities.

The work of the Spirit cannot be separated from the creative and redemptive work of God in Christ. Therefore, we need to be aware in ourselves and others that we are not creating pseudo-spiritualities which reflect more the searching longings of our contemporary culture than the transforming presence of the God who calls us into new life, but also into costly discipleship.

Embodiment

The gospel in human form

Our culture is tired of words. Little wonder that we have turned to images and symbolism. But finally these become reduced to words again as we seek to make linguistic sense of the world around us. Language after all is a fundamental mode of understanding.

Words have become particularly problematical for us because we are no longer sure that people mean what they say. An expression of concern may merely be cultural formality. The whispered promise of a lover may simply be a temporary flight of passion. The policy of the politician may only be the pretext for getting into a position of power. The seemingly good advice of a business colleague may in reality be a form of manipulation.

What makes all of this more difficult is the way in which our urban culture has decontextualized us. We are no longer part of meaningful primary communities and as a result relationships become tenuous and uncertain. We no longer journey with people over extended periods of time and hence have no basis for trust and certainty. This contributes to the uncertainty of the word.

In the sanctuary, the word has also become problematical. Not only do communities of faith have a huge turnover in membership and attendance, but religious specialists who run our churches are removed from most of their members. Moreover, proclamation is hardly a preferred form of receiving information in our contemporary culture. We want dialogue and participation and we want to be in a position where we can either take or leave what is being said.

The further difficulty is that the Church is no longer regarded as an authority in our society. It simply has an opinion alongside of many other values and positions in our pluralistic culture. The word of the Church cannot assume that it will receive an automatic, respectful hearing.

And yet, at the heart of Christianity is a message about the person and work of Jesus the Christ who in his life, death and resurrection made a new way of life possible. A way of life, available for all, which invites us into relationship with God, disempowers our old ways of being and acting and through the gifting of the Spirit gives a vitality of life in the shalom of God's kingdom.

The message, however, was an embodied message. It was a message carried by the integrity of the person. It was a word that was embedded in deeds of love and self-giving. It was the incarnate Word.

The Church needs to recapture the incarnation in its own

communal life. The Church as the continuation of the mission and ministry of Jesus is also to be a word that is rich in the deeds of welcome, grace, love and service.

Merton in one of his poems asks 'when a message has no clothes on, how can it be spoken'.[118] Changing the metaphor, we are asking the question, If a word has no embodiment can it be believed? The contemporary Church's answer to this question will be critical in its further demise or in the renewal of its life and impact on the wider culture.

Activism
The fragmentation of life

The various phases of life bring with them their own particular priorities and emphases. Childhood is the time of being protected, learning and wonderment. Early adulthood with its explosive energy is the time of pitting oneself against the world and making relational and career choices. When one becomes older one becomes more reflective and is happy in the role of empowering others rather than seeking to make one's own mark on the world.

These transitions in the rhythm of life also need to be understood in the way one lives one's Christian faith. There too, we see the move from early formation and learning through to various forms of activism leading in later life to a more reflective mode and a mentoring task.

Sadly, in some evangelical circles this movement of life is not understood or not appreciated. The Christian life is cast into a sameness and a regular movement from spiritual infancy to maturity. At the heart of this vision of the Christian life is an evangelical activism that knows little of the seasons of the spiritual life. It knows a lot about doing, not about being. It emphasizes action and knows little about waiting. It makes much of witness and underplays the role of contemplation.

Merton, coming from the Trappist tradition, speaks of an 'activist optimism in which there seems... to be a very notable amount of illusion'.[119] This applies well to some of the evangelicals I have in mind. In them, we find an unmitigated certainty that they know what God wants for this world and have set themselves the task of implementation.

The problem here is not the desire to witness to God's salvation in Christ and to serve the world. Rather, the problem lies in the failure to recognize that we both give and need to receive, that we serve and pray, that we act and wait. Moreover, we need to recognize that there are no straight lines in being God's witnesses in the world. There are periods of dryness, times of resistance, moments of uncertainty, as well as times of renewal and transformation.

It is not possible only to live the activist agenda. It will lead to burnout or disillusionment. It does not empower, but fragments. Mother Teresa's sisters are not committed to an activist agenda even though they faithfully and sacrificially serve the poorest of the poor. They are contemplatives in action. Worshippers on mission. And so must we all be.

This is not to suggest that we all engage the world in the same way and commit ourselves to the same ministry. But it does mean that our work in the world comes from being nurtured by God; being formed and sustained in Christian community; being empowered by the Spirit and being men and women of prayer. Moreover, that we know how to celebrate, dream of God's kingdom, bind up our wounded, laugh at the enemy and dance in the dark places of our world.

Impatient patience

Rediscovering a proactive spirit

Throughout many of the phases of the Church's long march, the Church has encouraged an unhealthy passivity and resignation. When life was difficult or the Church was experiencing oppression, the Church encouraged its members to bear the present difficulties empowered by the promise of heaven. The suffering of the now was to be tolerated in the light of eternal freedom and wholeness in the new heavens and new earth.

While it is appropriate to live in the light of eternity, it is not appropriate to embrace a fatalism regarding the present. Nor is it fitting that only the call to patience be heard. God's reign is not simply one of patience, but also one of shalom and transformation.

Merton echoes a similar concern. He notes, 'the word "patience" has been used and abused to cover every kind of inaction, foot dragging [and] double crossing'.[120] He had the racial problems of the USA particularly in view. But we can give this a much wider application.

There seems to be a strange notion afloat within the contemporary Church that social injustice can't really be tackled. We can proclaim the good news of the gospel to individuals so that they might come into a living relationship with Jesus Christ by the Spirit. But the gospel has no power regarding structural evil, social idolatry and injustice. The gospel in this view is a gospel of the heart and not of the transformation of the social order.

That this is a serious misreading of Scripture is evident in the exodus story, the laws of social justice in the Pentateuch, the prophetic tradition, Jesus' concern for the whole person and Paul's focus on the redemption of the fallen powers. Since so much biblical evidence can't be readily overlooked, I wonder whether the problem, in fact, lies elsewhere, namely in the middle-class captivity of the Church.

The middle-class ethos is one of suburban safety, relative prosperity and personal advancement. This flavours the largely middle-class Western Church with an inherent conservatism. The concerns for transformation are largely the concerns for others – the poor in our world and in the Third World. And for them we have token financial help, but not engagement, participation and identification. Thus despite information overload we remain largely uninvolved.

Yet the gospel calls us to an impatient patience. The message of the kingdom of God is a disturbing message calling us to love the neighbour and the enemy and to pursue peace, reconciliation and healing. Healing not simply for the individual, but also for our families, institutions and social structures.

BEING AND HOPE
The Search for an Eschatological Vision

So much of present-day Christianity is driven by sheer pragmatism. We seem to be preoccupied in the church sphere and in the spiritual life with what works best. In this, we are no different from our secular counterparts. They, too, are concerned with achievement and productivity and with discovering what works most efficiently.

Yet the Christian life, being part of the community of faith and practising the spiritual disciplines, cannot be understood in this way. All of this has to do with a very different orientation. The Christian life is a journey of faith and is lived in the midst of mystery.

What calls pragmatism into question is that the Christian faith is fundamentally eschatological in orientation. This has several layers of meaning. The first is that the Christian journey is not only for the here and now. It has a future in God's future – the formation of new heavens and earth. The second layer is that the Christian does not live by the resources of the present. Instead, the Christian lives by the in-breaking of the Spirit of God and in the light of God's future. The future of the redemption of all of creation and the healing of the nations does not only lie in a far-off future, God's kingdom has also come among us in the here and now.

The eschatological vision does not mean that the Christian begins to live only for the future to the degree that the present fades from view. It does not mean that we live awaiting the future eternal life while we neglect the world of economics, the arts and politics. It does not mean that we are only concerned with soul-saving because that has heavenly significance, and neglect the work of justice and social transformation.

The eschatological vision means something quiet different. While it does have God's final future in view, the eschatological perspective has to do with the in-breaking of God's reign, and living now in the light of God's healing of all things.

This has some important implications. The first is that an eschatological perspective is what transforms us because it is the fruit of God's Spirit breaking into our lives and reorienting us. The second is that this gives a vision of life different from that of our contemporary society. We do not live to the tune of society's dominant values, but to the dance of God's strange upside-down values which pursue the path of reconciliation, forgiveness, peace and the work of justice.

An eschatological vision inspires us to construe the present differently. We see the possibilities of God, rather than the self-achievement of humanity. We see apostolic sharing, rather than selfishness. Grace, rather than disempowering law.

Put differently, the eschatological vision allows us to live the dangerous memories of early Christianity and the contours of God's final future.

Marx of course was wrong. Eschatology does not dull us for the present, but rather empowers us for radical engagement. Merton understood this well. He believed that the strange monastic life of prayer, solitude, community was inspired both by early Christianity and by an eschatological vision. It was an anticipation of a life of full communion with God.

But Merton also cast his vision more broadly. Not only monasticism, but also a life of conformity to Christ, intentional community and the prophetic work of witness and social transformation reflects something of God's final future.

Eschatology is the fuel of hope. Not only does it empower us in the vision that a fuller future awaits us in the redemptive and healing work of God, but it also encourages us to live now what God's future will fully bring into being.

The new reality
Living in the light of eternity

There is something deadeningly ordinary about life. Caught in the cycle of birth and ageing, night and day, and work and play, we can live with monotonous regularity and without transcendent meaning. I know something of this way of life not only from my years devoid of faith and spirituality, but also since my conversion.

Of course, this need not be. Even the ordinary can be seen as a blessing from God. The daily rhythm of life is a structure that God provides for our well-being. Life itself, family, friends, society and work are all good gifts. Therefore, the ordinary need not be ordinary if it is lived in the light of God's presence and is celebrated with gratitude and joy. This view on life makes the ordinary sacred. But sadly, we all too often take the ordinary for granted, or even worse, despise what we have.

Thankfully, there is more to life than simply the ordinary. The extra-ordinary and the transcendent can also be a part of our daily existence.

Merton suggests to us that the person 'who loves God is playing on the doorstep of eternity'.[121] The word picture that he uses is not only a joyful one marked by simplicity and abandonment, but it also contains a profound spiritual truth, namely, that even here, on earth, we already experience something of the powers of the age to come.

In the enlightening and transformative power of the Word, the mystery of the sacrament, the exuberance or solemnity of worship, the intimacy of prayer, the revealing dream and the whispers of the Spirit, God playfully enters our normal reality as the God of surprises.

There is nothing frivolous about all of this. But it is playful. For God paints a different picture, creates a different melody and dances a different rhythm from the ones with which we are familiar.

When the God who is beyond us and our world touches our lives, we have the experience not only of differentness, but of a homecoming that gives us eternal security.

The historical task
Vocation in the light of eternity

Thomas Merton reminds us that 'to be in history is to have a task and a destiny, a difficult responsibility to oneself and to others'.[122]

Even though some find this sense of destiny, while many do not, this is not to suggest that one discovers this easily. We frequently wrestle with what it is that we should be on about.

To have a sense of destiny reflects a religious commitment. One believes that there is some ordained purpose to one's life. One also believes that this purpose is discoverable through some form of revelation and unveiling. And furthermore, one believes that one is called and empowered to embark on a particular vocation whatever the cost and consequences may be.

If one does not believe that to live this particular way has implications for eternity, then this way of life hardly makes sense. Inherent in this way of being is the idea that God in his sovereignty calls us and moves us in particular directions, which allows us to fulfil his purpose in our lives and thereby come to realize the purpose for our existence.

There is nothing automatic about any of this. God calls us in freedom, not with duress. And God uses the circumstances of our lives to mould and shape us. Even the seeming unwise choices that we may have made, God can redeem and utilize for his purposes in our lives. And the hurts and difficulties of life, as well as the gifts of family, friends, education and the workplace, God can take up in the orientation and shaping of our lives.

So then, what is our vocation in the light of eternity? Most fundamentally, in Christ we are called by virtue of the gift of faith, our conversion and the gifting of the Spirit, to be faithful to Christ and his gospel. This faithfulness will always outwork itself in love, obedience, witness and service. Whatever else we may do and be and wherever we may find ourselves this is our most fundamental calling. In living life this way we live with a view to God's kingdom and the things that finally matter in this life and the next.

Whether we live out this calling within the family or the work-place, at home or overseas, as primary childcare giver or engineer, within the service of the Church or in serving the wider community, this matters little. This of course is not to suggest that we should not seek God's direction about our daily work and where we should live. All of these things are important in fulfilling our purpose in life. But fundamentally, in loyalty to Christ we will seek to express his way, his values, his gospel in the daily task of priest or politician, artist or economist, as a parent or as a single person.

To have a sense of what God calls us to be and do in Christ is a most wonderful gift. So many people simply wander from one thing to another without direction and purpose. To be in God's kingdom is to have a kingly purpose. And that purpose is to love God, serve the neighbour and wash the feet of the world.

Imperfections
Weakness, sin and the triumph of grace

There have always been people who have dreamt of utopia, whether that be a political or a religious one.

It is little wonder that such dreams persist. We do have an archetypal memory of having been in the Garden of Eden. We don't need to rely on the faint traces of such a memory, however, to be reminded that we were banished from the garden and from the more immediate presence of God. We experience the pain of that loss every day. It is not surprising, therefore, that the more valiant and foolhardy among us believe that primal reality can somehow be recaptured.

Sadly, much manipulation, control and violence has been perpetrated in history in the pathetic pursuit of this unwinnable dream.

It has not only been political ideologies that have perpetrated the dream of a peaceful and just society. Religious groups have also trumpeted the present realization of the kingdom of God. Both religious communitarian movements and monasticism have sometimes given the impression that they can upstage paradise lost.

But in the most amazing communities, in the most saintly persons and in the most powerful renewal movements, sin and imperfection are present and evil sullenly lurks in the wings waiting to take centre stage.

The fact that evil will always mar our noblest dreams, best intentions and exciting experiments in human community does not mean that we simply give up and sink to the basest level. If the fullness of the kingdom of God cannot be captured any more than a small child can catch the wind, this does not mean that we no longer pray and work for all that God may yet give us.

Merton reminds us, 'but if the spirit of the world is always at work, nevertheless the Spirit of God does not leave his children alone and helpless in the darkness of the world'.[123]

While we never quite get there, we can come close. Utopia will always fail us, but we can build cooperative communities of faith. Sin will always be present in our lives, but we can live to God's glory and to the well-being of our neighbour.

In rejecting utopianism, we don't embrace cynicism. We can live in the joy of God's grace and the power of his Spirit.

Contemplation
The experience of eternity

I don't know about you, but much of my spiritual journey is structured on routine, commitment and various spiritual disciplines, including the experience of the community of faith with its preaching and Eucharist. There is a sameness about this journey and even a dullness that makes faith anything but a dynamic and joyful experience. Thus routine rather than intimacy is the dominant reality.

In my initial coming to faith as a teenager, intimacy with God was the overwhelming reality. I simply couldn't carve out enough hours from each working day to read Scripture, to pray and to be still with God. And of course I had not been taught anything about the practice of solitude. This desire to be in God's presence was totally spontaneous. When that initial experience began to fade and my faith went through its first existential crisis, I began to work at being with God with various degrees of success. What complicated matters was that I embraced a very activist faith where doing was celebrated and intimacy became more the longing and the dream.

Over the years, thankfully, all of this came a bit more into balance. Life was not only made up of service, but also of stillness. But my opening comments remain true. The more direct experience of God's presence is not the regular order of my day, even though I desire it to be.

Thomas Merton throughout his writings makes much of the contemplative experience. There are experiences of God's nearness that come as a result of the faithful exercise of the various spiritual disciplines. But there is also an experience of God that is the gift and the surprise. He calls this form of contemplation 'the light of God playing directly upon the soul'.[124]

While I cannot possibly know what Merton specifically means by this, I have had similar experiences. To find words for this is like reducing beauty to propositions and art to science. Even poetry is inadequate. But it has to do with an experience of love that holds and nurtures and renews us. There is a sense in which the burdens, fears and pains of life are caressed away and the wounded heart is made to sing with joy and adoration. There is a further sense of homecoming. The veil over our humanity is torn away. The barriers of distance, neglect and alienation are ripped away and there is the presence of embrace. This experience of God's gracious presence energizes and renews. It gives us new eyes with which to see ourselves, others and our world. And it empowers us for the service to which God has called us.

These experiences come and go. They are not of my doing, my searching or my piety or lack thereof. They are sheer gifts. But they reaffirm that we are made for God and are called to worship and enjoy him forever. These experiences prefigure the life to come in God's fully realized kingdom. As such they fill us with faith and hope and longing. There is more to come. We have only had a foretaste.

The road ahead
The long walk of faith

I am totally amazed. I had no idea that my life would turn out the way it did. But I am not sorry. In fact, I am deeply grateful. This is not to say that I have not made choices nor that I have not worked towards certain goals and objectives.

But the journey thus far looks nothing like its fragile beginnings, since no migrant kid who doesn't even finish high school could possibly imagine becoming a seminary professor.

But the rich texture of the journey is woven with more than simply one's professional development. Life is more than work and the road ahead has amazing contours. Merton puts it simply: 'I do not see the road ahead of me. I cannot know for certain where it will end.'[125] For him, life was an enriching writing career, although a Trappist monk, and a most untimely death.

All of this raises a myriad of questions. If life's journey is ultimately unpredictable, do I strive, plan, take initiatives and remain proactive? But surely life also has something to do with my genetic heritage and my socialization? Surely, training and vocational choices play an important part in the person I am becoming and the road that I take? At the same time, we have to allow for surprising openings and opportunities that come our way. And for the Christian, there is the dimension of God's providential care, guiding us in both expected, but also unexpected ways.

Since life itself is a mystery, it should hardly be surprising that the road ahead is unclear. And this can make us uncertain and insecure.

While more good than we had expected could come our way, greater difficulty may also be our lot. Sickness, redundancy, relationship breakdowns and a myriad of other problems may make the road ahead difficult or even unbearable. So how do we live towards an uncertain future, whether that be in terms of the macro picture or our personal destiny? I can only find one phrase: with quiet courage. A courage spawned not by the impulse of mastery, but by the humility of faith. A courage shaped by the faithfulness of God in the midst of our chequered life experience. A courage that believes that the God of the past and present is the God who welcomes and draws us into his future.

The road ahead is therefore not an abyss. Not a scary and empty place. The future frame is occupied by the One who has gone on ahead of us – the Christ of the Easter road. And he now beckons, welcoming us forward. Sometimes, his figure is disconcertingly vague and almost invisible. At other times, the One ahead is startling clear. It finally matters not, as long as we walk in his light.

Watch and wait; act and build?

Continuity and discontinuity

I grew up in the Reformed faith, which proudly saw itself in the lineage of its forebear, John Calvin.

The church's magazine had the symbols of a trowel and a sword. The trowel clearly stood for building – building the community of faith and also the wider community. What the sword stood for was more ambiguous for me. The truth? Power of rulership which was so characteristic of the old Christendom model? I was never sure.

But the first symbol was patently obvious. And the Reformed faith has always been clear regarding a Christian's dual calling. We are to serve the Church. But we also have a role to play in the world. We are to do God's good in our world. And this is the task not only for specially trained Christian workers, but for all God's people as lawyers, bakers, artists, mechanics, educators and those building and managing families.

Thomas Merton reminds us that 'building the kingdom of God in this world in preparation for the ultimate and eschatological revelation of the kingdom in eternity means in fact *building a better world here and now*'.[126]

Merton is clearly calling for Christian participation in the world. We are to act and build. He is not proposing that we withdraw from the world while we watch, wait and pray for God's final fulfilment.

I believe that Merton is correct. And I have attempted to live in the light of that understanding by building community, working in social welfare and working for social change.

But I think that important qualifiers need to be made. And one has to acknowledge that so little seems to change in the big picture in spite of the outpouring of so much Christian activity in our world.

Two sobering lessons regarding this point are that a decade and a half of significant work with drug addicts and homeless youth in a major Australian city only saw youth problems escalate. And the work of my friends among the urban poor in Metro Manila did not make a smidgen of difference regarding urban poverty.

This leads me to some theological fine-tuning.

I do believe that what we do, when it is in keeping with God's kingdom values, will last for all eternity. I also believe that there is some continuity between this world and the next. Those in Christ will participate in the world to come, and something of the glory of this world will be taken up in the future age.

But there is not only continuity, but also radical discontinuity. A transformed world. A whole new order. A whole new way of being. And this we cannot build, only God can bring that into being.

Thus in this world we do not build the Kingdom. But we build in faith with the kingdom of God in view. By the grace of God, we erect signposts that point to a new heaven and earth. And while we experience something of the fruit of God's kingdom among us, we, as wounded healers, long for the greater good. And hence we pray, Lord may your kingdom come and your will be done on earth as it is in heaven.

Homecoming

Finding God's rest in the place of service

Our Western way of thinking has led us to make distinctions and polarizations which fragment life. We separate work and play, and prayer and service. And we make major distinctions between this life and the next.

All of this has not served us well and we have lost the art of integration and seeing the connectedness of life. This is not only so with our daily work and life, but also in the way we understand and live out our spirituality.

One of the ways in which this polarized thinking impacts us spiritually has to do with the radical difference we make between this life – our earthly existence, and the life to come – our heavenly existence. The one almost has nothing to do with the other, except that the former is a preparation and trial run for the life to come. Thus this life is a kind of proving ground for making our way to the next level of existence.

The idea of proving ground has all kinds of implications. One is linked to the reality of suffering. Some hold the idea that the more we suffer here, the more purified and holy we will be in preparation for the life to come. The other is linked to service. The more we help others, the greater our future reward will be. The further idea is linked to blind faith. We live life as best we can in a difficult world, hoping that God is somehow with us even though he seems to be so terribly absent. So we try as best we can and hope that the next life will be more blessed than this vale of tears.

However understandable these thoughts may be, they come more out of an unhealthy dualism rather than out of the biblical vision. Dualistic thinking makes a too radical difference between the soul and the body, creation and redemption, nature and grace, and heaven and earth. The biblical story, in contrast, not only celebrates both, but makes important interconnections. Both body and soul need God's healing presence. And God is with us now as much as he will be with us in the life to come, even though then we will know God more fully and see him more clearly.

Thomas Merton in one of his poems puts it like this: 'come, in my labour find a resting place, and in my sorrows lay your head'.[127] It is in the midst of life that we need the nurturing presence of God, not simply at the end of the journey. It is in the now that we want to taste God's kingdom, not only in the future age. It is in the midst of our weary and broken world that we long for God's healing and not only in the new heavens and new earth where all will be reconciled and made whole.

The present is a time of homecoming, not only God's eschatological future. Thus we don't only wait for what is yet to come. We may celebrate and dance in the now, for God's salvation has come in the death and resurrection of his Son and the joyful Spirit drives home to us the blessings of Golgotha's hill.

God-centred

Living in the present for the future

Merton makes a startling assertion. He writes, 'it was because the saints were absorbed in God that they were truly capable of seeing and appreciating created things, and it was because they loved him alone that they loved everybody'.[128]

What is being suggested here is that when we truly know and love God and are loved by him, this will powerfully affect everything that we do, including the way we live our lives in the day-to-day world.

Before we pursue this key idea a little further, I believe that a number of qualifiers are in order. The first is that people who do not share in the Christian faith are capable of loving and appreciating the world of nature and the world of human creativity. In fact, probably more so than some Christians. The Renaissance person has shown a greater appreciation of art and beauty than the Reformation person.

Second, there are counter-examples. The long Christian story of some two thousand years does not always reflect the above ideal. Christians have failed to hold the dove of peace and instead have taken the sword to hand. Nor have they always been the good stewards of God's earth. This list can easily be extended.

A third qualifier is in order. The above quote could imply some form of spiritual elitism. That only spiritual giants, the saints who live this deep life with God, are able to live exemplary lives in the world. But I don't believe that this is what Merton is suggesting. He is saying something quite different, namely, that when we turn our faces towards God, we need not turn from the world.

This can and should be put much stronger.

God and world should never be played off against each other. God not only created the world and providentially sustains it, but God has entered and continues to enter human history. God has truly come among us and seeks to weave his story with our story.

So when we turn to God in worship, prayer, listening and solitude we do so as individuals, but also as a people belonging to families, communities, places of work and to our world. These, we may and should bring with us. God is open to our praise and the cry that comes from the pain of our world.

So in one sense, there is no pure contemplation of God. We encounter the God who is for us and who has entered the human fray. In a similar way, we do not come to God as disembodied spirits, but as singles or marrieds with our history, training, sexuality, giftedness and dreams.

To truly love and know God does not remove us from our world. Nor does the eschatological future that God has for us. To know God draws us to show God's love and care for the neighbour. To believe in the world to come means that we also long, pray and work that the future world will become more apparent among us.

Put differently, to know and love God helps us to see our world more carefully. Love helps us to see truly and moves us to action that is inspired by God's shalom, rather than by our understanding of what is helpful and beneficial.

Non-arrival

The never-ending quest for wholeness

No matter how much we long to be closer to God, and how much we seek to be more prayerful and more spiritual, the best we can do is to make regular steps towards the fountain of God's grace. For that is the only place where we can continue to be forgiven, renewed and empowered. This is a most humbling confession, especially since we long for so much more.

In the human breast there beats the longing for ultimacy. And in the long course of history we have seen the development of philosophies, ideologies and social change movements that were based on utopian dreams. Both fascism and communism are merely two contemporary manifestations of that impulse.

Religions exist primarily to meet the human need for final answers. They speak about the beginnings of our world, the meaning and purpose of life, hope in the face of suffering, and life beyond death. They speak of an ultimate Being to whom we can turn in worship and prayer and from whom all life and meaning comes.

Christianity forms no exception to this general observation. However, the major features of this faith take on particular hues and colours. The God of the Bible is the God who enters history to redeem the oppressed. In Christ, this God comes in weakness. In the shame of the cross, salvation is won for us. And the meaning of life lies in the faithful following of Jesus.

There have been times when Christian groups have over-emphasized the nowness of a fuller Christian experience. Through holding particular beliefs, or through being part of a particular group, or through participating in certain spiritual practices, these Christians believed that they could enter a state of perfection and blessedness that set them apart from others, made them special to God and made them a special sign of God's kingdom.

These ideas continue to be attractive, even in our post-Christendom world. To be different in our culture of sameness and to be special in a world of mediocrity, are appealing options. In a world of relativism and loss of meaning, to have the certainty of faith, the blessings of the Spirit and the fullness of the spiritual life, are powerful draw cards.

Yet we have to be careful at this point. These powerful appeals may be the spurious certainties of the insecure. Our quest for ultimacy may simply be the blind diversion of an inability to face the pain and woundedness of our life, and the brokenness of our world. It's a grasp for transcendence without having faced the realities of our vulnerability, our rootedness in the world and the persistence of our sins and the sins of others.

The overwhelming testimony of the saints of the Christian faith is that the more they grew in sanctity the more they realized how little they knew God, how sinful they still were and how far away the ultimate point of their journey was still. Thomas Merton forms no exception to this broad observation. He writes, 'there have been repeated failures . . . like holes appearing everywhere in a worn-out garment'.[129]

For some, this may be a most disappointing testimony from a man radically converted to Christ, from a monk living a life of prayer and contemplation and from a Christian writer whose books have inspired millions. Yet it is an appropriate testimony for Merton and for all of us. The final witness is not our spiritual progress and sanctity, but the grace of God freely given and carrying us in the journey to wholeness.

The quest for spirituality and wholeness can so easily be a narcissistic self-preoccupation. Our growth, rather than God's glory, becomes the spurious focus. And our sanctity, rather than the redemption and transformation of our world, is our dominant concern. This clearly is not the focus of the gospel, where the good news is what God continues to do in us and with us and not what we have achieved.

The spiritual quest
A vision for this world and the world to come

Many years ago I befriended in Australia an English wooden coach builder. His trade had all but died out and he had moved 'down under' to find a new life and vocation. He had turned his hand to building old version homesteads which maximized the use of timber, including whole logs.

John often talked with some pain about the loss of a world associated with coaches and the skills associated with it.

This loss of old worlds and old skills is intrinsic to our modern world with its vast and impressive technological changes.

But I wonder whether other things have also been lost as we continue the transition to a world whose contours remain malleable and essentially futuristic.

That we have lost a culture of Christianity is obvious. No longer do we have a world where the values of those within the community of faith approximate those in the wider community. While there are those who loudly lament this fact, this state of affairs may in fact be a blessing to the Church as it seeks to recover a vitality in keeping with its first-century beginnings.

But in many ways the contemporary community of faith is more wedded to the values of our modern world than to the strange values of the Galilean teacher.

This is nowhere more evident than in the present quest for a spirituality which rather than emerging out of a deeply biblical vision is much more a recycled self-fulfilling individualism.

Thomas Merton, addressing an earlier Western audience, made the observation that 'an emptiness that is deliberately cultivated, for the sake of fulfilling a personal spiritual ambition, is not empty at all: it is full of itself'.[130] He may well have been speaking to our contemporary age!!

The spiritual quest that is oriented towards creating greater self-awareness, integration and well-being is not without its value, but it pales in the light of the biblical vision.

The heart of this vision has first of all to do with a transcendent relationship with God the creator and redeemer who calls us into fellowship and intimacy. Moreover, spirituality without the grace and empowerment of God's Spirit is like a pool without water, a car without an engine, a sunset without the sun, a frame without a picture.

Furthermore, biblical spirituality is sustained and expressed in community. It is not just about me. Its concern is me *and* others. It's a relational spirituality which, while it knows the blessings of solitude, also knows the grace of community and mutuality. This is a spirituality which gives and receives within the context of a community of worship, learning, nurture, care and accountability.

Finally, a biblical spirituality knows the reality of servanthood and hears and responds to the cry of the poor. Spirituality not only knows God and neighbour, it also knows the cry for justice.

If spirituality draws us to God, it also draws us into God's vision for this world and the world to come. And since that vision is one of shalom those who least experience it should be our ongoing concern.

Kept by God

God's providential care for the whole creation

There is so much that is good about our world. The wonder of birth, the blessing of family, the privilege of work, institutions that serve us in a variety of ways, the creativity of art and music, and the beauty of special places and nature.

What is especially amazing is that despite the dysfunctionality of so much of modern life, friendships are made, community is built and people continue to care and serve. There is love in our world even though violence and hatred are also on the horizon of our experience.

Thomas Merton also expresses his surprise. 'It is a miracle', he writes, 'with so few people praying on this earth, that the world has any virtues at all.'[131] That it does is a sign of God's beneficence and grace. Somehow, we are kept by God, and life goes on with women and men of goodwill making valued contributions.

God's mysterious and sovereign care for the world of humans and the created order does not relegate human responsibility to the sidelines. On the other hand, it does not all depend on us, for if it did our world would soon fall into chaos.

The fine interplay between God's initiative and human responsibility is a puzzle we will never unravel. What we do know is that God and his grace is greater than us. What we also know is that God invites us to full participation in his purposes.

What the biblical story makes clear is that God made all things and upholds the created order by his power. The story also makes clear that God is at work in the human story, the movement of history and the social order that makes life liveable and whole.

In the human story God both upholds and interrupts. There is nothing monochrome about God's activity. And in this complex activity, God by his Spirit sustains the good and subverts evil through the conversion of perpetrators. God's activity is committed to both maintenance and transformation. This will always make God's involvement in our world paradoxical.

God's paradoxical presence in our world calls us to faith and contemplation. We need to learn to see and hear. We need to discern the movement of God's Spirit in our times in both Church and world and in the deepest recesses of the human heart. And having partly seen and heard we are called to action and participation.

In all of this our eyes are on God, rather than on the world. But our eyes are not on the absent God, but on the incarnate God mysteriously made manifest in our tired world. In this God we hope. This God we serve.

Worship

Celebrating the love and greatness of God

There is a singular ordinariness to life. This is even true for the high achievers and the adventurers. Even if there were more projects to complete or more mountains to climb, one does finally become satiated. This sameness to the journey of life is also true for the Christian. Living, working, loving, resting, and failure, disappointment, weakness, are part of the texture of all of our lives.

This, of course, does not deny the high points that are the signs of unexpected grace. The gift of faith. A wonderful friendship. Marriage. A new job. Renewal in the Holy Spirit. The list is potentially endless. But even these high points are quickly swallowed up by the inexorable rhythm of daily life.

The secret of life is not to live for the high points, nor to despise the daily journey. Rather, the secret is to celebrate the good, unexpected and undeserved. And to bring the daily journey with its sameness and disappointments into the ambit of God's presence.

One way to do this is regularly to read, reflect upon and pray the Psalms. Whatever we may think of the Psalms, they have served as a voice for Jews and Christians throughout the generations. Their almost universal language of hope and despair, abandonment and homecoming, failure and reconciliation, has served the Church through the millennia.

Thomas Merton writes, 'we bring to the Psalms the raw material of our own poor, isolated persons with our own individual conflicts and sufferings and trials (and) we throw them all into the fire of Christ's love'. Rather than denying what is happening to us in the ordinary and difficult realities of our lives, we bring all this to God in prayer and surrender. Sometimes, we may even bring these things to God with angry words. But bring them we may and must.

It is precisely in the surrender of the ordinary to the God of all grace that the glimmers of hope may appear. Transcendence in a long and tired journey. Peace in a persistent turmoil. Grace in the long stretch of guilt. Joy in the midst of difficult circumstances. A word of direction in a long and seemingly aimless silence.

Merton in continuing to speak of our interaction with the Psalms acknowledges praise leading 'to ecstasy', the flash of 'dark lightning' and 'the silence of heaven'.[132] It's as if the world beyond breaks into our probing faith, our tenuous hope, our fitful prayers. This becomes the undeserved and unexpected turn-around that makes life full and empowers us for the journey.

When these graces come our way we cannot but celebrate life and worship our Creator and Redeemer. In the amazement of this grace we express our gratitude and finger the edges of eternity. It is the God with us now that fills us with hope and gives us the courage for the journey onward.

On the other side of far
A spirituality of hope

Even though we build families, develop friendships, join communities of faith and create institutions of cooperation and service, we are not so good at the art and politics of solidarity. We seem to be better at the doubtful achievement of fragmentation. When we practise the former, we partake of the movement of God. When we all too often play out the latter, we express the human capacity for competition and polarization.

This doubtful dialectic is very much a part of the human condition. We move between creativity and chaos, generativity and decay. And even though we fall frequently into the latter, the desire for the former remains and often becomes even stronger.

While our failures may bring us to despair, they can also bring about the opposite result. They can move us to try again, to hope again, to love again, to live again. And while woundedness may lead us to further brokenness, we may also receive grace to forgive and see the growth of new gifts and abilities in our lives.

Thomas Merton in one of his poems expresses the following: 'we are two spectres seeking each other; finding the other far'.[133] Here we see a similar dialectic; seeking and absence, closeness and distance, nearness and removal.

This observation brings us to a strange mystery in human experience. We come to the extremity of our lostness, and are suddenly found. We come to the end of our strength, endurance and resources, and somehow find new energies. We have waited endlessly for the promised arrival of a particular person, gift or position, and when we were ready to close down on our last vestiges of hope, the door springs open.

This is frequently the experience of faith and the spirituality of hope. This is the other side of far. Instead of the expected abyss, there is the lowered drawbridge. In the silence of God, there is the hand that holds us. In the dark night of the soul, there are the glimmers of light. And in the absence, are the whispers from the edge of eternity.

This side of far brings us to the end of our resources and abilities. It brings us to the desert. To the empty place. To the place without companion or consolation. And while we expect the other side of far to be more of the same or even worse, we unexpectedly find ourselves in the oasis of God's mysterious hand and his generous provision.

To experience this is to taste something of the world to come. It is dining at the banqueting table before all is ready. It is the consolation of God in the place of desolation. And it reverses everything that we had expected. As such it is a taste of the reign of God. It is dipping our toes in the shalom of his kingdom. It is being kissed by God.

Trust

Relying on the God who is greater than us

We all experience times and situations where we are full of worries, if not about one thing then about another. While worry may be justified, it is usually less than helpful. Although there may be times where worry becomes translated into a particular intervention, whether that be prayer or practical help. Of course, when that happens it ceases to be worry.

Worry and the accompanying anxiety that it brings is very much a part of life, because in so many ways we are powerless. We are subject to forces and circumstances that can affect us, and those whom we love, for the worse. Illness, economic difficulties, personal crises can come our way, and when these impact on our loved ones we may worry all the more.

It is clear that worry is not absent from the spiritual life. In fact, the opposite is often the case. The 'saints' of the faith worry about their prayer life, their sanctity, their walk with God and the quality of their service. Many such Christians are always taking their spiritual pulse and are always wondering whether they are good enough or do enough.

When this occurs the message of God's grace is slipping from view. Moreover, we become too much the focus and who God is and what he will do in us and for us recedes into the background.

Thomas Merton in his journal notes, 'some people are worried about the community and sometimes I am tempted to be also. But no, we are in God's hands.'[134] It is so easy to be worried about our life together. It matters little whether that be the community of family, an intentional Christian community, a community in mission or the community of workplace. The reason for our concerns is that community is inherently fragile and requires much nurture and care. But while we may serve well in the community, we do have to trust God with our life together. Finally, community is a gift of God's grace.

Trust is a gift and disposition that pulls us out of ourselves and our ability and prowess, into the arms of the Other. Trust empowers us to live in a transcendent and eschatological way. While trust is born out of faith in the faithfulness of the Other, it is often triggered through our powerlessness and inabilities. Trust is expressed in the cry: I can't; you, O God, must!

Merton had to trust that the Trappist community of which he was a member was ultimately God's doing and that God could sustain and empower its life together. We are called to similar positions of faith. We too have to entrust ourselves and all that we have to the God of grace. Similarly, we need to entrust our families, communities, ministries, businesses and social institutions to God's care and empowerment.

This does not mean that we don't work hard at preserving, building and renewing the groups that we are a part of. But we need to remember that life, our communities and the movement of history are so much bigger than all of us. It is God who needs to sustain us and give the increase, and when this occurs we live beyond ourselves in the shadow of eternity.

Faith

Looking for God's new in our old

It is possible to look at the world with the eyes of wonderment. The welcoming hello of a child; the flash of a flock of lorikeets; the hue at dusk; the wash of the blue Pacific on white sand; the gaze of a lover; the joy of birth; the miracle of healing; the celebration of family and friends at the meal table. The list is endless. Life is full and calls for wonderment and thankfulness.

But we also see life with eyes of pain. There is loss, misunderstanding, hurt, betrayal, abuse. There is sickness and tragedy. And everywhere we see the script of inequality and injustice.

While we may wish that wonderment would predominate, it is the painful vision of life that most often swims into view. The good and the bad never get dished out equally.

But it is also possible, while looking at life with the eyes of wonderment and pain, to use our eyes of faith. Merton writes, 'my faith is an eschatological faith . . . I can even now "see" something of the glory of that kingdom'.[135] In the midst of life's daily realities with its joys and difficulties, it is possible to be graced with the Spirit's gift of faith.

The gift that I am talking about here is not the charism that believes in God and his word. This is important and foundational. But it's another gift that I have in view. It is the charism that draws the future in the present. It believes in healing when there is sickness; peace in the midst of violence; forgiveness when there has only been hatred; reconciliation when a community has been deeply divided.

This gift of faith sees something of God's final world breaking into the present. This is not a case of mind over matter, or a flight into idealism. Nor is it something that we work up. It is sheer gift. And it may come at the most unexpected times.

This faith may see the conversion of a loved one; a new mission begun; a tired institution renewed; a new movement birthed. This faith traces the new contours of the Spirit. It sees the new even when the old still dominates.

This visionary faith is the premise for all forms of renewal. While reorganization may simply be the reshuffling of the old, renewal is the in-breathing of new life inspired by the Spirit of God.

When these things happen – and happen they do – then we are at the edge of eternity. The undeserved new wine of the kingdom gushing into the dry places of our personal, social and institutional existence. There are never enough buckets to hold the water of life. And sadly we soon focus on the utensils and not on the content. Little wonder that the renewing Spirit has to visit us again and again and the gift of faith needs to be received by us.

Beyond Christendom
The search for new ways of being the people of God

The journey of the Church of God in history has never been a smooth and uniform march. From its pristine beginnings as the Jesus movement and the Pauline house churches, the Church has had a chequered history. It has reflected an exemplary self-giving as well as an arrogance that used the sword to transform the soul.

In our time, the Church is neither sacrificial nor arrogant. It is lost. Its days of privilege and status in the general society have long gone and it finds itself insecure and uncertain in the pluralisms of our contemporary world. In response to this, most Christians are bewildered, some are ardently striving for a return to the good old days, while others have simply capitulated to the ethos of our time and have reduced their faith to a psychology of personal meaning and well-being.

Merton, echoing the writings of Karl Rahner, believes that the way forward is for us to discover new ways of being the people of God. He writes, 'in the Diaspora situation the Christian as individual may precisely be asked a heroic faith with little or no human support'.[136] Basically what this means is that the present-day Christian will need resources for faith and life that come from a different place to that of the Christendom model.

The implication of this is a reconfiguration of what it means to be a Christian and what it means to be Church. In Christendom, the Christian was a loyal member of the society and a faithful participant in the life of the Church. Fundamentally conservative, the Christian of that time saw himself or herself as a supporter of the structures of society and a resister of the forces of change. But this stance has proved futile. The powerful forces of change unleashed by the Enlightenment, with its rationalization of life, swept all before them, including the Church of conservative convenience.

Christians now find themselves as a minority movement in a post-denominational age where old loyalties no longer matter. As a result, they have to find a new way. Ironically, finding this new way does involve looking back especially to the pre-Constantinian era where the Church was a minority movement in a hostile Roman empire.

What may be common to then and now is the discovery of a faith that is tested in the dark and hard places. A faith that is formed over a much longer period of formation. A faith that knows the heart cry of captivity. A faith that is more deeply prayerful and much more attentive to God.

For some this sounds scary. It makes faith more fragile and spirituality more vulnerable. But to walk this road may bring us much closer to the shalom of God than our present consumerism and programmatic Christian approach which is tiring but not transformative and gives few answers to the critical questions of our day.

Resurrection

God's surprise in the midst of death

It is true that so much of life has to do with the sheer joy of receiving. It is a fact that so much is given. Life. Family. Friends. Education. Resources. Work. Leisure. All these things come from God's beneficence along with the blessings of grace, forgiveness and the empowerment of the Spirit.

But in life we also experience an often fearful stripping away. This is different from the experience of renunciation. The latter is a voluntarary act where through the impulse of faith in the call of God we embrace the service of asceticism. Here we open our hearts, hands and homes in order to bless others through relinquishment and self-giving. Renunciation is an exodus spirituality where we are called out of our own concerns and preoccupations to share ourselves and our resources with others, including those outside of the community of faith.

The experience of things being stripped away from us is something that happens to us. It is not something we choose to do. Finally, life will be stripped away from us as we enter the desolation of death. But other things are also taken away. Health. A career. A relationship. A reputation. A vision of life. A fruitful ministry. In these experiences we are subject to pain, confusion, loss and frequently a sense of abandonment.

Our contemporary culture is not too enamoured with the idea of renunciation. While it may be admired and applauded, it is really rejected as being foolish, given the profound self-preoccupation that lies at the heart of Western values. But our age fails to face this stripping-away process. We do everything we can to deny or avoid difficulty and pain. We believe only that things should be given, not that things can be taken away.

And yet, this process lies at the very heart of the mystery of faith. While our society lauds rationality, achievement and productivity, faith calls us to a different vision of life. In this vision the strong have to face weakness, the rich their poverty of spirit, the capable their blinding pride, the righteous their sinfulness.

What is stripped away is not our humanity but our idolatries, not faith but our false hopes, not meaning but our illusions.

Thomas Merton in one of his poems expresses this as follows: 'and lay me in my three days' sepulchre until I find my Easter in a vision'.[137] A strange prayer, indeed! Who wants to embrace death in order to find life? And yet, this is the heart of the gospel and the mystery of faith.

Stripped of all, followers, disciples and life itself, Christ becomes the life-giver. The broken One becomes our healer. The naked One, clothes us in the righteousness of God. The rejected One brings us into the embrace of the Father. The dying One, becomes the source of life for all humanity.

If God's way in the world is unfolded in that peculiar way, then we, who in faith are bound to the foolish wisdom of God, can hardly expect that we will experience God's action and presence in a fundamentally different way. We will have to embrace our many small deaths in the light of Christ's great death in order that we also experience God's resurrection life, the life of eternity.

The impulse to life
Reaching for the beyond

Life has to be lived in acceptance and gratitude. And life has to carry and sustain us. In this sense, life is a gift which is accepted in the way it comes to us.

But in another sense, life is something we reach for. I deliberately do not use the phrase 'strive for'. Too much striving or the impulse to power is not life-giving. It is in this quest for self-determination and self-fulfilment that we somehow over-reach ourselves. We try to make everything happen and consequently become destructive in the way we live.

Life has to be received, but we can also reach out for the more. But this more is to be God's good, and this also needs to be given and received by us. Even in our reaching out, we are still the recipients of God's grace and good gifts.

Merton writes, 'in the darkness he remained famished for light, in chaos his spirit still thirsted for order and peace, and in his nonentity he could not help but to aspire to being, to spiritual liberty, to a true identity'.[138]

There are many ways in which we can read this. One is that no matter how dark and difficult things may become for us and for the human race, we will always long for and move towards the better and the more beautiful. This places an optimistic interpretation on the human condition. The other way of reading this is that in our darkest moments God's grace and goodness will be there for us, moving us into his light.

While I prefer the latter reading to the first because it magnifies the grace of God, there is a third way of reading this statement. Rather than seeing this as an ontology of being, namely, that there is always the human impulse to the good and better, this passage speaks of the dialectic of life and the ethics of reversal.

What I mean by this is that the 'curse' of darkness can lead to the blessing of light. Put differently, the greater the pain of the one reality the more we reach out for the opposite. But to put that even stronger, the action of God is the ethic of reversal. Death leads to resurrection. Rejection to reconciliation. The burden of the law to the freedom of grace.

It is this understanding of the rhythm of life that makes our contemporary values so inadequate and false. These values speak of me at the centre when God should be there so that the One who is the core of all things will bless us who are so small and marginalized.

Furthermore, these values speak of having as happiness, and fail to understand that only empty hands can truly be filled. These values speak of power and control, when blessing lies in vulnerability and servanthood.

At the very core of life lies this strange dialectic where the surprise rather than the prediction becomes life-giving. Of course, the Gospels do know something about this – the first shall be the last and the last first.

Invitation to dance
Celebrating God's present future

Dancing and the life of faith at first appearance do not belong together. The life of faith is serious business since it has to do with our eternal destiny. Dancing belongs to the more frivolous aspects of life.

While in no way wishing to undermine the nature of the life of faith, there is something profoundly joyful and even frivolous about it.

I am talking here not of a frivolity marked by bawdy behaviour, nor of an escapism from the daily regulated and demanding responsibilities of life. I have something quite different in view.

Dancing belongs to the life of faith and the spiritual journey as surely as prayer, the Lord's Supper, teaching and worship.

By dancing I do not simply mean doing a jig to a certain kind of music. But I mean celebration, partying and having fun. And I have done more of this when working in the suburbs of despair in the First World and the slums of injustice in the Third World than in living a more prosaic middle-class lifestyle.

It is true that the poor know how to celebrate, party and have fun. They do it with zest and zeal. And they do it when the occasion demands it and more often when there is no occasion at all. And while there may be a certain amount of escapism at play here, that is not the basic story. The poor celebrate to affirm life in the places of degradation and death. Celebration is the expression of joy in the gift of life that God continues to give.

I believe that dancing also has other important purposes in the journey of faith.

First of all, it gives us sacred moments in which we detach from the bitter-sweet realities of life. To create distance from the monotonous sameness of everyday life, and celebrate, is a form of transcendence that is but a mere foretaste of the ecstatic nature of the age to come when we enter into God's full shalom. Dancing is, therefore, an experience of sabbath.

Second, dancing helps us to gain new perspectives on life's difficult realities. The daily grind not only tires us, but begins to orchestrate the consciousness of our inner world. Our social landscape begins to paint the contours of our soulscape. We begin to become our difficulties. And the persistent power of the god of injustice begins to decimate the sacred places of faith in our inner sanctuary. While dancing by itself is never enough and we need renewal through the spirit of hope, celebration carries us long enough into another mode of being so that we can see the familiar world with new eyes – eyes of faith and hope in the God of the exodus.

And finally, when we really think about life in the light of faith, there is every reason to dance. God has given us life. God has come to us with gifts of grace. There are the signs of God's kingdom even in the places of injustice. And while we struggle, we need not give way to despair, for the power and the glory do belong to the God who accompanies us in weakness in our present journey.

Merton is right, therefore, with his reminder, 'the fact remains that we are invited to forget ourselves...(to) cast our awful solemnity to the winds and join in the general dance'.[139]

Thomas Merton: A brief chronology

1915	Born 31 January in Prades, France to his father Owen Merton, an expatriate artist from New Zealand, and his mother Ruth Jenkins Merton, an American with a Quaker background.
1916	The Mertons move to the USA to live with Ruth's parents in Douglaston, Long Island.
1921	Ruth Merton dies of cancer when Thomas is six years old.
1922	Owen and the young Thomas spend some time in Bermuda where Thomas attends elementary school.
1923	Return to Douglaston.
1925	Owen returns with Thomas to France.
1926	Thomas enters the Lycée Ingres in Montauban, France.
1928	Thomas is taken to England to stay with his uncle, Benjamin Pearce, and attends Ripley Court school.
1929	Thomas is further educated at Oakham, an English boarding school.
1931	Owen Merton dies of a brain tumour, leaving Thomas an orphan at the age of 16.
1933	Thomas wins a scholarship to Clare College, University of Cambridge to study modern languages. His time there is brief and his guardian sends him to his maternal grandparents in Long Island, USA.
1935	Enrols at Columbia University to study literature and develops a close friendship with Mark Van Doren, a faculty member.

1938	Completes his BA at Columbia and prepares for work on an MA thesis. On 16 November Thomas is baptized into the Catholic Church.
1939	Completes an MA thesis on 'Art and Nature in William Blake'.
1939–41	Thomas teaches English at St Bonaventure College (now University) and contributes to various newspapers and magazines in pursuit of his dream to be a writer. He applies unsuccessfully to join the Franciscan order.
1941	Spends time as a volunteer in Friendship House, Harlem, founded by Baroness de Hueck. Enters the guesthouse of the Cistercian Abbey of Gethsemani in Kentucky as a postulant.
1944	On 19 March, Merton makes his simple vows.
1944–49	Publishes four volumes of poetry: *Thirty Poems*, *A Man in a Divided Sea*, *Figures for an Apocalypse* and *Tears of the Blind Lion*.
1947	Makes solemn vows on 19 March. *Exile Ends in Glory* is published, a book on the life of Mother Berkmans.
1948	*The Seven Storey Mountain* is published. This book makes Merton a household name. It tells the story of Merton's life up to his entrance into the monastery.
	The Spirit of Simplicity published by the Gethsemani monastery.
1949	Ordained on 26 May to the priesthood within the Cistercian order.
	Seeds of Contemplation is published, as well as *The Waters of Siloe*, a history of the Trappists.
1950	*What Are These Wounds?*, based on the life of St Lutgarte of Aywiues, is published.
1951	Merton has *The Ascent to Truth* (original title *The Pillar and the Cloud*) published. This book is Merton's reflection on the works of St John of the Cross. The

same year Merton becomes responsible for the training of monks for the priesthood within the monastery.

1953   Merton produces *The Sign of Jonas* based on his reflections of life in the monastery. This book, like *The Seven Storey Mountain*, is highly autobiographical. A meditation on the psalms, *Bread in the Wilderness*, is also published.

1954   Merton writes *The Last of the Fathers*, a series of reflections on St Bernard of Clairvaux.

1955–65 Is master of novices at the Abbey of Gethsemani.

1955   *No Man Is an Island* is published, in which Merton explores certain themes of spirituality – solitude, silence, recollection, asceticism and sacrifice.

1956   Merton writes a series of eucharistic reflections published under the title of *The Living Bread. Praying the Psalms* is published.

1957   *The Strange Islands*, a book of poems, is published, as well as *The Silent Life*, a study on various forms of monasticism.

1958   *Thoughts in Solitude* is published.

1959   *The Secular Journal of Thomas Merton* is published, as well as *Selected Poems of Thomas Merton*.

1960   Merton's *Disputed Questions* is published, dealing with literary, theological and social issues. *The Wisdom of the Desert*, a selected translation of some of the sayings of the desert fathers, is also published and the small book *Spiritual Direction and Meditation* sees the light of day.

1960–   Merton begins to write on socio-political issues, including the atomic arms race.

1961   *The New Man* is published. *New Seeds of Contemplation*, an expansion of the earlier *Seeds of Contemplation* (1949), is published, as well as *The Behaviour of Titans*, an extended prose poem.

1962   *A Thomas Merton Reader*, edited by Thomas McDonnell, is published (a revised edition came out in 1974).

1963   *Life and Holiness* and *Emblems of Season of Fury* are published. Merton receives the medal for Excellence from Columbia University.

1964   *Seeds of Destruction* is published. Merton receives an honorary LD from the University of Kentucky.

1965   *Seasons of Celebration*, reflections on the liturgy, is published. Also *The Way of Chuang Tzu* comes into print. Merton edits *Gandhi on Non-Violence* and begins living permanently in the hermitage within the Abbey of Gethsemani grounds.

1966   *Raids on the Unspeakable* and *Conjectures of a Guilty Bystander* are published.

1967   *Mystics and Zen Masters* is published.

1968   *Zen and the Birds of Appetite*, *Cables on Ice* and *Faith and Violence* are published.

        In the early part of this year Merton makes a number of short speaking trips to California, Albuquerque, New Mexico and Alaska. Leaves for Asia on 15 October, travelling to Calcutta, Dharamasala, Darjeeling, Singapore and finally Bangkok, where on 10 December he gives an address to a meeting of Asian monastic superiors. That afternoon he is found dead in his room, reportedly from being electrocuted by a faulty fan. He is buried on 17 December at Gethsemani.

1969   Merton's novel *My Argument with the Gestapo*, and *Contemplative Prayer* and *The Geography of Lograire* are published.

1970   *Opening the Bible* is published.

1971   *Contemplation in a World of Action* and *Thomas Merton on Peace* are published.

1973   *The Asian Journal of Thomas Merton* is published.

1976	*Ishi Means Man* is published.
1977	*The Monastic Journey* and *The Collected Poems of Thomas Merton* are published.
1978	*A Catch of Anti-Letters* is published.
1979	*Love and Living* is published.
1980	*Thomas Merton on St Bernard* is published.
1981	*The Literary Essays of Thomas Merton* is published.
1985	*Eighteen Poems* is published.
1985–94	Five volumes of Merton's correspondence are published: *The Hidden Ground of Love: Letters on Religious Experience* and *Social Concern* (1985); *The Road to Joy: Letters to Old and New Friends* (1989); *The School of Charity: Letters on Religious Renewal and Spiritual Direction* (1990); *The Courage for Truth: Letters to Writers* (1993) and *Witness to Freedom: Letters in Time of Crisis* (1994)
1988	*Thomas Merton in Alaska* and *Wood, Shore and Desert* are published.
1989	*Thomas Merton: Preview of the Asian Journey* and *'Honourable Reader' – Reflections on my Work* are published.
1992	*Springs of Contemplation* is published.

Notes

1   *The Intimate Merton*, p. 218
2   *The Living Bread*, p. 9
3   *The Sign of Jonas*, p. 215
4   *The Sign of Jonas*, p. 75
5   *Conjectures of a Guilty Bystander*, p. 20
6   *Seeds of Contemplation*, p. 142
7   *The Seven Storey Mountain*, p. 43
8   *Waters of Siloe*, p. 16
9   *Disputed Questions*, p. 34
10 *Love and Living*, p. 41
11 *The Sign of Jonas*, p. 191
12 *No Man is an Island*, p. 128
13 *Conjectures of a Guilty Bystander*, p. 224
14 *Seeds of Contemplation*, p. 49
15 *Life and Holiness*, p. 21
16 *The Sign of Jonas*, p. 236
17 *No Man is an Island*, p. 122
18 *The Sign of Jonas*, p. 256
19 *No Man is an Island*, p. 43
20 *The Asian Journal of Thomas Merton*, p. 338
21 *No Man is an Island*, p. 19
22 *Disputed Questions*, p. 82
23 *Disputed Questions*, p. 61

24   *Loving and Living*, p. 35

25   *Entering the Silence*, p. 311

26   *Love and Living*, p. 145

27   *Disputed Questions*, p. 65

28   *The Seven Storey Mountain*, p. 295

29   *Life and Holiness*, p. 159

30   *Seeds of Contemplation*, p. 34

31   *Conjectures of a Guilty Bystander*, p. 137

32   *The Seven Storey Mountain*, p. 277

33   *Contemplative Prayer*, p. 25

34   *Seeds of Contemplation*, p. 66

35   *No Man is an Island*, p. 116

36   *The Sign of Jonas*, p. 296

37   *The Power and Meaning of Love*, p. 92

38   *The Sign of Jonas*, p. 30

39   *The Sign of Jonas*, p. 287

40   *The Living Bread*, p. 18

41   *Contemplative Prayer*, p. 19

42   *Contemplative Prayer*, p. 43

43   *No Man is an Island*, p. 50

44   *Thoughts in Solitude*, p. 32

45   *Disputed Questions*, p. 111

46   *Spiritual Direction and Meditation; and What is Contemplation?*, p. 85

47   *The Waters of Siloe*, p. 297

48   *No Man is an Island*, p. 81

49   *Thoughts in Solitude*, p. 19

50   *Seeds of Contemplation*, p. 146

51   *Seeds of Contemplation*, p. 160

52   *Contemplative Prayer*, p. 76

53   *The Waters of Siloe*, p. xxiii

54   *The Waters of Siloe*, p. 116

55   *Seeds of Contemplation*, p. 43

56   *The Living Bread*, p. 10

57   *Entering the Silence*, p. 398

58   *Seeds of Contemplation*, p. 82

59   *The Monastic Journey*, p. 34

60   *Preview of the Asian Journey*, p. 36

61   *Entering the Silence*, p. 351

62   *The Sign of Jonas*, p. 312

63   *Life and Holiness*, p. 43

64   *Seeds of Contemplation*, p. 152

65   *Seeds of Contemplation*, p. 208

66   *Seeds of Contemplation*, p. 56

67   *Zen and the Birds of Appetite*, p. 30

68   *The Courage for Truth: Letters to Writers*, p. 29

69   *No Man is an Island*, p. 244–45

70   *Contemplation in a World of Action*, p. 41

71   *Seeds of Contemplation*, p. 64

72   *The Sign of Jonas*, p. 281

73   *Spiritual Direction and Meditation; and What is Contemplation?*, p. 30

74   *Seeds of Destruction*, p. 255

75   *The Silent Life*, p. xiii

76   *The Collected Poems of Thomas Merton*, p. 201

77   *Preview of the Asian Journey*, p. 42

78   *Conjectures of a Guilty Bystander*, p. 97

79   *Seeds of Contemplation*, p. 124

80   *Conjectures of a Guilty Bystander*, p. 119

81   *Seeds of Contemplation*, p. 111

82   *Contemplation in a World of Action*, p. 126

83   *Emblems of a Season of Fury*, p. 82

84 *Contemplation in a World of Action*, p. 145

85 *Conjectures of a Guilty Bystander*, p. 325

86 *Thoughts in Solitude*, p. 56

87 *Thoughts in Solitude*, p. 85

88 *The Sign of Jonas*, p. 49

89 *On Peace*, p. 124

90 *The Power and Meaning of Love*, p. 64

91 *Conjectures of a Guilty Bystander*, p. 120

92 *Seeds of Contemplation*, p. 140

93 *Opening the Bible*, p. 81

94 *The Asian Journal of Thomas Merton*, p. 329

95 *The Collected Poems of Thomas Merton*, p. 756

96 *Emblems in a Season of Fury*, p. 70

97 *Life and Holiness*, p. x

98 *Life and Holiness*, p. 57

99 *The Sign of Jonas*, p. 155

100 *The Sign of Jonas*, p. 132

101 *No Man is an Island*, p. 228

102 *Contemplation in a World of Action*, p. 91

103 *The Monastic Journey*, p. 28

104 *The Monastic Journey*, p. 44

105 *The Sign of Jonas*, p. 279

106 *Contemplation in a World of Action*, p. 132

107 *No Man is an Island*, p. 70

108 *The Monastic Journey*, p. 35

109 *The Waters of Siloe*, p. 23

110 *The Seven Storey Mountain*, p. 370

111 *Conjectures of a Guilty Bystander*, p. 218

112 *The Sign of Jonas*, p. 150

113 *The Courage for Truth: Letters to Writers*, p. 6

114 *Conjectures of a Guilty Bystander*, p. 86

115 *Opening the Bible*, p. 41

116 *Seeds of Contemplation*, p. 156

117 *Seeds of Contemplation*, p. 101

118 *Emblems of a Season of Fury*, p. 49

119 *A Vow of Conversation*, p. 51

120 *Seeds of Destruction*, p. 309

121 *The Sign of Jonas*, p. 126

122 *Opening the Bible*, p. 71

123 *The Waters of Siloe*, p. 147

124 *Spiritual Direction and Meditation; and What is Contemplation?*, p. 99

125 *Thoughts in Solitude*, p. 83

126 *Disputed Questions*, p. 102

127 *The Collected Poems of Thomas Merton*, p. 36

128 *Seeds of Contemplation*, p. 18

129 *The Intimate Merton*, p. 207

130 *Contemplative Prayer*, p. 94

131 *The Secular Journal of Thomas Merton*, p. 120

132 *Bread in the Wilderness*, pp. 87, 101, 111, 125

133 *The Collected Poems of Thomas Merton*, p. 958

134 *Entering the Silence*, p. 174

135 *A Vow of Conversation*, p. 116

136 *Seeds of Destruction*, p. 197

137 *The Collected Poems of Thomas Merton*, p. 95

138 *Seasons of Celebration*, p. 205

139 *Seeds of Contemplation*, p. 230

Bibliography
Works by Thomas Merton

The Ascent to Truth. London: Hollis & Carter, 1951

The Asian Journal of Thomas Merton (eds Naomi Burton, Brother Patrick Hart and James Laughlin). New York: New Directions, 1973

Bread in the Wilderness. London: Hollis & Carter, 1954

The Collected Poems of Thomas Merton. London: Sheldon Press, 1977

Conjectures of a Guilty Bystander. New York: Image Books, 1966

Contemplation in a World of Action. Garden City, N.Y.: Doubleday, 1971

Contemplative Prayer. London: Darton, Longman & Todd, 1969

The Courage for Truth: Letters to Writers (ed. Christine Bochen). New York: Farrar, Straus & Giroux, 1993

Disputed Questions. New York: New American Library, 1960

Emblems of a Season of Fury. New York: New Directions, 1963

Entering the Silence: Becoming a Monk and Writer. The Journals of Thomas Merton, Vol. 2 (ed. Jonathan Montaldo). San Francisco: HarperSanFrancisco, 1996

'*Honourable Reader': Reflections on my Work* (ed. Robert E. Daggy). New York: Crossroad, 1989

The Intimate Merton: His Life from his Journals (eds Patrick Hart and Jonathan Montaldo). San Francisco: HarperSanFrancisco, 1999

Life and Holiness. New York: Herder & Herder, 1963

The Living Bread. Kent, UK: Burns & Oates, 1956

Love and Living (eds Naomi Burton Stone and Brother Patrick Hart). New York: Harvest/Harcourt Brace Jovanovich, 1985

The Monastic Journey. London: Sheldon Press, 1977

The New Man. New York: Noonday Press, 1961

New Seeds of Contemplation. Norfolk, Conn.: New Directions, 1961

No Man is an Island. San Diego: Harcourt Brace Jovanovich, 1955

On Peace. London: Mowbray, 1976

Opening the Bible. London: Allen & Unwin, 1972

The Power and Meaning of Love. London: Sheldon Press, 1976

Preview of the Asian Journey. New York: Crossroad, 1989

Raids on the Unspeakable. Kent, UK: Burns & Oates, 1964

A Search for Solitude: Pursuing the Monk's True Life. The Journals of Thomas Merton, Vol. 3, 1952–1960 (ed. Lawrence S. Cunningham). San Francisco: Harper, 1996

Seasons of Celebration: Meditations on the Cycle of Liturgical Feasts. New York: Farrar, Straus & Giroux, 1965

The Secular Journal of Thomas Merton. New York: Farrar, Straus & Cudahy, 1958

Seeds of Contemplation. Wheathampstead, UK: Anthony Clarke, 1961

Seeds of Destruction. New York: Farrar, Straus & Giroux, 1965

The Seven Storey Mountain. London: Sheldon Press, 1961

The Sign of Jonas. New York: Image Books, 1954

The Silent Life. New York: Farrar, Straus & Cudahy, 1957

Spiritual Direction and Meditation; and What is Contemplation? Wheathampstead: A. Clarke, 1975

Thoughts in Solitude. New York: Harcourt, Brace & Co., 1958

A Vow of Conversation: Journals 1964–1965 (ed. Naomi Burton Stone). New York: Farrar, Straus & Giroux, 1988

The Waters of Siloe. New York: Harcourt Brace, 1949

Zen and the Birds of Appetite. New York: New Directions, 1968

Secondary Bibliography

Carr, A., *The Search for Wisdom and Spirit: Thomas Merton's Theology of the Self*. Notre Dame: University of Notre Dame Press, 1988

Furlong, M., *Merton: A Biography*. San Francisco: Harper, 1980

Hart, p. *Thomas Merton: Monk*. New York: Sheed & Ward, 1974

Kramer, V., *Thomas Merton: Monk & Artist*. Kalamazoo: Cistercian Publications, 1987

Mott, M., *The Seven Mountains of Thomas Merton*. Boston: Houghton Mifflin, 1984

Nouwen, H., *Thomas Merton: Contemplative Critic*. San Francisco: Harper, 1981

Pennington, B., (ed.), *Towards an Integrated Humanity: Thomas Merton's Journey*. Kalamazoo: Cistercian Publications, 1989

Shannon, W., *Silent Lamp: The Thomas Merton Story*. New York: Crossroad, 1992

Wilkes, P., *Merton By Those Who Knew Him Best*. San Francisco: HarperCollins, 1984